go ask ogre

go ask ogre

LETTERS FROM A DEATHROCK CUTTER

jolene siana

HOW CAN I STOP FEELING SAD?

t is natural to feel sad when someone you
e dies. You miss them. You may feel lonely.
u may feel confused too. Most people—not
t children—feel the same way when someone
y love dies.

Sadness is something like the
en you hurt yourself. At firs
ch. But it will hurt less each d
u think it will be gone. Then
think about the person who h
eeling sad.

Right now you are trying to
bout death. This will take som
way. It helps to ask questions.
uch to tell your family and
eel. It helps most of all not to
re sad, don't pretend you are
ad, don't try to make yourself

WRITE
ME !

© 1987 P.A.T.—Ward

i can't go on.
back door—cox

PROCESS
LOS ANGELES

MR. Kevin Ogilvie
4oNETTwerk Productions
BOX 330
1755 Robson Street
Vancouver, B.C.
Y6G 1C9
CANADA

airmail
FIRST, FAST AND RELIABLE
par avion

guess who?

This book is a work of non-fiction.
Some names have been changed.
Self-injury warning: content could be triggering.

Go Ask Ogre © 2005 by Jolene Siana.

Process
P.O. Box 39910
Los Angeles, CA 90039

Page 26 photo © Nicole Smith
Page 143 photo © Big Glenn
Page 155 photos © Ali Isaacs

www.goaskogre.com
www.processbooks.net

Editor: Jodi Wille
Book Design: Gregg Einhorn
Copyeditors: Felicia Daniel, Susan Jonaitis
Production Assistance: K. C. Kyle

ISBN: 0-9760822-1-7
      9780976082217

10 9 8 7 6 5 4 3 2 1

Printed in the USA

For Bob & Ogre

What we call our destiny is truly our character, and that character can be altered. The knowledge that we are responsible for our actions and attitudes does not need to be discouraging, because it also means that we are free to change this destiny. One is not in bondage to the past, which has shaped our feelings, to race, inheritance, background. All this can be altered if we have the courage to examine how it formed us. We can alter the chemistry provided we have the courage to dissect the elements.

—Anais Nin

Disturbed Thoughts —
Welcome to my Life

The Darkest Year

14 February 1987

Nivek Ogre,

I'm Jolene. I'm 17. I'm a senior at an extremely boring school. It's packed full of heavy metalers. Do you like heavy metalers? Sorry to say but I don't get along with them too well. I hate this school. I graduate on June 11, one day after my 18th birthday. I was born in 1969. When were you born? I got in a car accident 4 days after I got my license in December. My insurance is quite high and my mother was yelling at me this morning because she got the statement in the mail. My mother hates me. I hate hate. My grandpa died in June and my grandma died in October. Death is so mysteriously cool, but I miss them deeply. Make sense? I like Death in June—the band, that is. I bought their album because I liked the way the cover looked. I like the way you look. I'm so bored. I'd like to scream. Just scream and see how the people in my classroom react. But I can't, you see, because I'm not really that kind of person. I'm not obnoxious. I like to make scenes sometimes, but most of the time I like to just look really gothic and artsy and go out and have people laugh.

I want to be a journalist. I want to go to England. I want children, but not for a while. I'm not sure about marriage. I'm going to the Toledo Art Museum today. I like art. I can handle looking and admiring it every once in a while, but mostly I like creating my own works of art.

~~

I'm in ceramics class right now. Hmm…I haven't a single picture of you. I've only seen the video for "Dig It" and part of "Smothered Hope." I only have two records: *Mind—The Perpetual Intercourse* and *Remission*. I didn't know offhand what "perpetual" meant. My teacher enlightened me. Did you know that there is a definition for "punk rock" in the dictionary?

PUNK ROCK—a form of hard-driving rock music characterized by an extremely bitter treatment of alienation and social unrest. That is so hilarious. Do you realize I haven't done anything in this class this hour? I've been writing you and looking up words in the dictionary. I love dictionaries. I like proper grammar. I've been told that I have proper grammar. I hate when people say "ain't" and words like that. It truly irks me. Some sophomore guy keeps writing me letters. He's a jock. I'm not into jocks really. I have a stomachache. I haven't eaten in quite some time. Vivarin makes me jittery. My teacher doesn't like Bauhaus. She lets us bring music to class to listen to. She's cool!

26 February 1987
10:09 a.m.

I'm supposed to be drawing, but I really don't feel like it at this moment. I'd rather write to you. I hope you're reading this letter. I'd hate it to lie in a pile of fan mail. I suppose I'm a fan. It's so bright in here.

I have a lot of pen pals. I really ought to be writing one of them, but I'm not. I'm writing to you. I doubt if I'll get a response. That's all right. One of those heavy metalers that I complained about earlier just wrinkled a page that I wrote to you! I'm mad!

I'm in yet another art class. I have 4 art classes—3 independent study and 1 ceramics class. The only other classes I have are American Government and English, easy enough.

Well, I'm not hungry anymore. I had a bagel for lunch. It was kind of dry.

I'm tired—still. I'm home, but can I sleep? No. It's just not possible. My mother hates me. I hate myself. Life really pisses me off, you know? I'm on the verge of doing something. It's not funny. I'm about to do it. One thing. It will only take one thing before I just explode. I hate it. Why am I even living? Why can't I be dead? Why

was I born? I'm going to do it. I know it's going to happen. I don't want to do it, but it's going to happen no matter how much effort I give to stop it. I don't want to die, but I don't want to live. I can't handle it. I miss my grandparents so much. What's going to happen to me? There's nothing I can do. Everyone "normal" thinks I'm weird. I used to be in the "in" crowd. I changed my style, and people think I'm a devil worshiper or something. No, I'm not. I'm human.

It's just a feeling, I get sometimes
a feeling, sometimes, and I get frightened
just like you, I get frightened too.
—The Sisters Of Mercy

If this is not Nivek reading this, whoever you are, please don't think I'm psycho. Will you write me back? That's a pretty stupid question. I need a friend. Matt is my friend. Good friend. He lives in Michigan, though, and I can't call him because I owe $33 for last month's phone bill. I wish I could talk to him.

I don't feel well, but I'm not in a suicidal mood anymore. Please write back. Please. I'm really spazzing out or something. I'm an only child. Only child is short for Lonely child. I live with my mother. It's a love/hate relationship. Rarely love. What is love? Look at this poem that I wrote. I don't remember when I wrote it, all I know it that it's really stupid.

Today is ugly
I hate it so
Why? You ask
Well, I don't know.
My mother hates me,
Grandparents are dead
A burning pain inside my head
My hair's not right
He bothers me
Today I tripped and hurt my knee
Enough of this, my fingers ache
So now I'm going to take a break.

Pretty hilarious? Pretty stupid!
I suppose I ought to go.
I love you too.
Jolene

27 February 1987

I'm at school again. Boring. I'm in a pretty awful mood. I hate this mood. It's not a good mood and it's not a bad mood. It's an in-between mood. In-between moods are confusing because you feel like your existence means nothing. No one cares if you're here, and no one cares if you're not.

My mother really hates me. She's always insulting me, and that really bothers me. She's so closed-minded. It's pathetic. I really hate closed-minded people. The same guy that hit my foot yesterday practically knocked my books over today.

I can't wait to move. I have a few ideas on what I can do this summer. You see, my aunt made a deal with me. If I don't get pregnant or hooked on drugs or alcohol, then I'll get $1000 for graduation. My mother made the same deal with me. Great. Anyway, I want to go to Europe so badly! If I can't do that, I'm going to travel the U.S. I'd like to visit all of my pen pals.

Can you believe Andy Warhol died? That's sad. I almost died a few times. When I was about four years old, maybe three, I almost drowned. It was at this one beach. I went with my mother's friend and her son Carl. There was a little shallow section for younger kids. Everyone was swimming in a circle. I wanted to swim in a circle so badly, the next thing I knew I was…well, I remember what I thought was a photograph. I saw about 5 men (paramedics) holding me, trying to get all of the water out of me. They all had short "proper" hair and they were wearing white shorts. Now, when I look back on it, it seems like I had an out of body experience. I doubt it. I look so awful today. I was supposed to go to demerit class but I didn't.

Did you ever have an imaginary friend? I did. Her name was Becky Levy. She was really tall and really skinny and she had long straight hair. It was brown and she had bangs. She always wore green pants and a long-sleeved orange shirt. It didn't have any buttons or anything.

I'm listening to "Love" from *Mind TPI*. I love that song. I can only listen to one more song because this one guy wants to play the Beatles. They're not so bad. I can handle them. Why are we here? What's music going to be like in the future? Drugs, who needs them? I'm not on drugs. I just took Vivarin because I was really tired and depressed. Now I get really tired and then I get really hyper. I don't feel well. I have to go down to the girls' dean because my stupid airhead counselor never explained to her that I'm in an independent study art class, not study hall. If they put me in study hall I'll be so mad.

1 March 1987

You'll never guess why the dean called me down. She was curious about my change. Black hair and all. She wondered if I'm into devil worship, drugs, etc. I laughed. What I thought was going to be a big ugly talk turned out to be somewhat pleasant. Anyway, big deal. I'm in English class right now. I hope that someone is reading my letters. They are much too artsy to go to waste. I love art.

I bought a Christian Death album earlier this week and I don't like it as much as the really gloomy stuff. Are you an atheist? I'm supposed to be Catholic. I went to a Catholic elementary school and whatever but now I'm not too sure about what I believe in. Who cares? My hands are all dry. I'm going to go home, take a shower, clean my room and…try to make my mother love me. I wish my grandmother were alive. I really miss her. After my grandpa died I was with her all the time. She was so great. I have this scary belief that there's no afterlife and I'll never see her or my grandpa ever again. I've never seen my father. My mother never married him. I guess he was some exchange student. She was with him at a party or something. It doesn't matter. My grandpa was like a father.

uoy evol I

Jolene

8 March 1987

I'm excited about tomorrow. Why? Because I just happened to find another Skinny Puppy album. Actually, I'm not sure if it's an album or not. All I know is that it's called *Bites*. I'm going to get it tomorrow. I can't wait. This week isn't going to be all that bad. Tomorrow: new Skinny Puppy; Tuesday: my friend Jackie is having a party; then this weekend I'm going to stay in Ann Arbor. Maybe I'll even get some information on Skinny Puppy in the mail. It's been almost 2 weeks since I first wrote to you. Peter Gabriel was in Toledo a few days ago. I don't really like his new stuff. His old stuff is really excellent though. I don't feel well. My back hurts. Am I a chronic complainer or what? I want to meet you! I also want to meet this guy Porl from Britain that I write to. He's so sweet.

Shirley Temple was a really talented little girl, wasn't she? I'm not going out with Mike anymore. We got into an argument the other night. No big deal. I didn't like him much anyway. I'm still hooked on that stupid user John. I'd better be going.

Razor Blades & Bullets.

Jolene

19 March 1987

Nivek,

Well, I didn't go to school yesterday. Yes, again. My ex-boyfriend Will called at 1:30 a.m. That's nothing unusual, but he asked if he could come over today. I told him he could. It's so strange, because it seems like he's infatuated with me or something. Whereas last year it was the other way around. He asked me why I talk to him like I'm better than him. I couldn't help but laugh! If he weren't so "normal," I'd go out with him again. Unfortunately he's a jock-prep. You know, Mr. Popularity in high school 3 years ago, and he can't let go. Oh well. I told him that he could come over, but he'd have to wear something black. He was all excited. I think it's funny. I hope he doesn't expect anything (physically) because there's no way he'll get "anything." What we had was last year and that's over. I am however going to introduce him to Skinny Puppy.

I know John will be at the show on Sunday. I pray that he will say hi to me. I haven't seen him for one month and six days. He doesn't like me. Well, he likes me sometimes. He used to really like me. He used to call me. Whatever. He's not my usual type. He has long stringy bleached blonde hair. I liked it better when it was black. He's tall, he's thin, and he's good-looking—well, in an odd way. He acts really cute—kind of like

~John Weills

Razzle in *Suburbia*. He's just a user though, and I don't like users. I really like (here is where I got in trouble for writing to you). My teacher said, "Letter writing isn't doing a damn thing for your future!" Whoa! Blew me away. Actually this letter could be doing something for my future, that is, if you write me back.

[Editor's note: On April 14, 1987, Jolene received a hand-written letter from Nivek Ogre in the mail. Respecting Ogre's wishes, the contents of the letter shall remain private.]

14 April 1987 (Journal)

Nivek Ogre wrote me! Wait—stop everything! Every-ever-everything! The best thing in the world has happened to me. Remember Nivek Ogre? Remember Skinny Puppy? He wrote back!

Nivek Ogre is also known as Kevin Ogilvie. I still can't believe he wrote me! I never wrote to him about how hot he is and I never told him that I'm completely obsessed with him. I only wrote things about myself! I'm so glad he wrote. It's so strange that he wants to meet me! Nivek Ogre wants to meet me!

My room

15 April 1987

Hi Ogre,

Last night Will called me at four a.m! (Late or early?) I couldn't believe it. I mean, I wouldn't have been upset if I liked him, but seeing that I don't care much about him, that was not a very clever thing for him to do. I'm tired and shouldn't be. I drank three cups of coffee. That's my drug lately. The Mission are playing in Detroit tonight. I wish I could go. This may sound strange, but the only means of me getting my feelings out is on paper to you.

I hate being hurt, but I realize it's a part of life and I suppose I can handle it. I don't like who I am sometimes. I don't like who I am sometimes. I don't like who I am sometimes. I don't like who I am sometimes. I don't like who I am sometimes…but sometimes I do.

I have this really big secret that I'll never tell anyone. It's awful and I hate it. Why do I want to cry right now? Perhaps it's this song. "Giving Ground" by The Sisterhood.

I haven't cried in awhile. Quite often I've wanted to, but a few weeks ago a girl from Toledo was riding her bike and she was hit by a semi-truck and killed instantly. I guess all that was left of her was her head, an arm and two legs. That is too sad. That makes me want to cry so badly. She was only 17. I'm 17. Then someone had the nerve to put a gigantic picture of her mangled bike and her sneakers on the front page of the newspaper. Talk about morbid. The semi driver tried to stop. I guess it was mostly her fault. She was riding through moving traffic, but all of that pressure and guilt and remorse. It's all on him. I'm sure he'll never be the same again. I'm glad the driver didn't get cited. I guess the paramedics and policemen were getting sick. They just couldn't handle it. Who could? It's been haunting me. I miss my grandma and grandpa. They're really and truly gone forever. I'll never ever see them again.

I cut my wrist. I didn't mean it. It's not a bad cut. It itches. My picture is coming along. It's not completely done though. Strange. I wore all white today and people seemed to be extra, extra nice to me. Figures. Society is so predictable.

I got 2 un-sats today. "Unsatisfactories"—one in American Government class and one in English. So what. No one will be in school tomorrow because it's prom day. Why aren't I going to prom? What a joke. I went last year. I hated it.

I really like old people. I feel so bad when an old man or woman comes into my restaurant to eat alone. I assume they're widowed. I seriously want to adopt grandparents. They're so cute. I'm strange. So what.

My mother always calls me ugly. I was telling Matt and he said, "I don't know why. I think you're quite pretty." That made me feel happy. Will called me. I was surprised. It wasn't like 3:00 in the morning. He was being really nice and not perverted at all.

I am so angry I could scream. I usually don't care about stupid rumors, but this is too much! I'm sure. Kevin and Diane have been spreading gross, disgusting, repulsive rumors about me. Some friends. While I was yelling at Diane, Lindy came over and started a scene by saying, "You don't even care about my life, you don't even care about me." Then she blamed Diane for getting Lindy and me into arguments, so Diane called Lindy a bitch and almost hit her. Then, if things couldn't get worse, that metal chick Tawny came out into the hall and gave her two cents about the situation. Then Brandy came out and Diane started yelling at her.

I just stood there laughing because it was the only way I could possibly handle it. Now, I ask, is it really that hard to understand why I want to be antisocial?

I hate today. My project for the art show looks ugly, but guess what I'm calling it: *Social Deception*. My portrait has a few good qualities, but it looks funny. I really can't wait to yell at Kevin. Watch, he'll deny it. I found out he told his whole first hour that Lindy and I are lesbian lovers! Scream. Everyone just LEAVE ME ALONE! I'm sure, after that happened I came into the art room and this guy started teasing me by saying that he only likes me when I wear white—otherwise I'm ugly. What a fucked up day. As you can tell, I'm angry again. I have so much rage in me, I'm about ready to explode. I swear, I am! No, we are not lesbian lovers, but Lindy is so needy she acts like she's my girlfriend! That's scary. I wish I could get out of here. I actually screamed. I screamed into my jacket. Everyone heard me. I was embarrassed. Now I'm overhearing people talk about the girl who got hit by that semi.

Do you like the color of dried blood? I do. I don't really like pain. I don't like pain of any sort. Mental pain, physical pain. Pain! I also don't like this pen. It says "Howard Johnson" (as in the motel) on it. I took it when I was on vacation. I need another vacation. You can't always get what you want. I love my grandparents. Abcdefghijklmnopqrstuvwxyz. Have you ever heard that song by Big Bird? It's cute. They played a joke on me at the YMCA. I hated junior high. I'm tired. I'm alive. I'm dead. I'm bored. I'm imperfect.

I'm about ready to do it. No big deal. People kill themselves everyday. I'd be another number. I hate numbers, and right now, at this very minute, I hate my life.

My friend Natalie told me that Skinny Puppy are supposed to play at St. Andrews in Detroit. Detroit is only 45-60 minutes from Toledo. I'm going to go, but I doubt if I'll get in because it's 18+. My friend Jonathon will probably be going. He's the one who reminds me of you. I was really surprised that he didn't have any of your records. He seems like, well, he dresses like you're his idol. Actually he's <u>really</u> into Sisters of Mercy, The Mission, and Bauhaus. Who cares? The point is that you are the reason that he and I are friends, thank you.

I don't think my mother is coming to the art show. I'd kind of like her to, because she seems to think that I'm extremely disliked. She thinks my teachers think I'm "weird." I'd like her to see that they don't (well, they don't appear to).

12:47 a.m.

I just got home from the chicken slaughterhouse. I hate working at a fast food place. I asked for a part-time job, not a second home.

It's 2 a.m. and I have to get up at 6 a.m. Can I do it? By my letters I thought you'd think I'm psycho or something. I wasn't about to write you and be phony. If you do think my letters are psycho, that's because I wrote them. You know, I can understand what you mean about not being any certain religion. I was raised Catholic, but I find myself not believing in all that they stand for. I haven't gone to church forever but I still pray. I pray and I don't even know what I believe in. I know one thing. I like to think that there is a superior being that can control certain things. Sometimes I just don't know. I suppose I'm just a twisted little girl. Whatever.

Well, before I get into bed and try to sleep, I'd just like to say thank you for writing, because to me, one of the most precious gifts one can receive is knowing that someone took time out of their life to think of you. It's wonderful!

﹏

16 April 1987

Nivek,

Everybodyknowsitswrong.

Today is such a cemetery-like day. It's rather gloomy and quite windy. I like it. Want to hear something strange? I bought 9 albums today, none of which were

Skinny Puppy. I couldn't wait to get home to listen to them. Ninety some dollars on records then I come home and listen to Skinny Puppy. I wish I could fall asleep.

Guess what? I have this big blood blister in between my thumb and index finger. It's so ugly. I'm going to pop it tomorrow. I am getting some use out of my new records. My friend wants me to tape Alien Sex Fiend for her. Do you like them? Why am I so depressed this evening? It comes on just like that. Out of nowhere. I'm down again. I'm sad. I have an ugly blood blister on my hand. Well, my friend Matt from Michigan just called and I'm in a much better mood. He's going to see your show in Detroit and he's going to look for someone who will let me borrow their ID. Good.

＊＊

I had a pleasant chat with my mother. She made me listen to some of her music and I made her listen to some of mine.

＊＊

Just trying to touch you but never to hold you
—Red Lorry Yellow Lorry

＊＊

I'm so tired but I can't fall asleep. The past 2 nights I've had the most disgustingly morbid dreams. They've been about my grandparents. In the first one I found my grandfather dead in his house.

?*%# $!!!!! …etc. I blew a fuse. The whole apartment is pitch black! My clothes are in my mother's car, and I can't listen to music! Scream!!! I'm really upset at this moment. I'm sitting in my room, lit by a white scented candle, writing to you. I wish my mom would hurry up and get home! Our electricity doesn't work and that means no music, and I was planning on staying in and being antisocial tonight.

10:19 p.m.

Well, I'm being close to antisocial. My mom went over to her friend's house and I was too scared and too lonely, so I'm over at Diane's house watching a movie. No electricity. I hate having no electricity. No music hell.

＊＊

18 April 1987

Nivek,

I had the most incredible urge to write to you, therefore I'm writing. Chocolate. Rotten chocolate. I'll tell you about it.

I'm in a quite <u>depressing</u> mood. At this moment, I'm in Albany, N.Y. We're staying at my friend's parents' house. They're smoking pot, and it smells like what I'd imagine rotten chocolate smells like.

Anyway, I'm really sad because tomorrow is Easter and our family is celebrating and I'll be away. Also, my grandparents are dead and I truly miss them. It was about a year ago when my grandfather started getting sick. I miss him so much. I—oh, I don't know. I want to cry, but crying just depresses me even more because I think that I'm feeling sorry for myself. Guess what? I don't have any real friends. Sure, I have a lot of friends, but there is not one person who truly understands me. Not like a friend is someone who has to understand you but... Lindy in my eyes is flaky, possessive, boring, intelligent, nice, and self-centered. She gets attention by telling everyone that she hates herself and that she wants to die. I have only been hanging around with her for about a year and she acts like she owns me. She expects me to take her everywhere that I go. She thinks (well, thought) that I only like to hang out with "scene people." Wrong. I started hanging around with Diane who is completely NORMAL, outgoing, happy, caring, open-minded. Oh, did I forget to mention that all Lindy does is go around saying how AWFUL everything is, etc.?

Well, I'm tired and depressed (because my batteries are dead) and fearing that I'm boring you, so I'm going to bed.

21 April 1987

Nivek,

Hello. I haven't written in the past few days because it's been pretty hectic around here. My mother is really getting to me. The other night at about 1:00 a.m. she yelled at me because my ex-boyfriend kept calling me. Then I had a dream that I told her about my past with him. She got really angry. We kept arguing, then one day we were getting along all right and she left for awhile and when she came home she turned around and said, "I'm leaving you," and she pulled out this big knife, really big, with a rigid blade. She hit my neck, then threw me on the living room floor and put the knife on my neck and put her hands on the two ends of the knife and cut my head off! It was so real. I remember thinking in my dream, "I'm dead. God wants me now. There's nothing I can do," then (my dream was in color) it turned to black, gray, and white. It was like a television screen and it said something like, "You are here." SCARY. I woke up crying. This morning my mother kept telling me how much she hates me and that she hopes I get in a car accident so that she won't have any worries! I don't need that. I have a bad enough self-image—her saying things like that doesn't help much! Whatever! I'll be eighteen in 3 months! I can't wait! Oh, I got your album the other day. *Bites*. Great music. No lyrics, no pictures. Depressing!

I'm in last hour. Believe it or not, we're not doing anything. Everyone is talking about graduation. It's going to be really thrilling (sarcasm). This stupid jock who claims that he has perverted dreams about me is saying that he'll be crying at graduation. Not me! I'll be so happy to get out of here!

30 April 1987
2:20 p.m.

I'm in a very hating mood! I'm hating. I really don't care about anything at this moment and that's scary!

11:41 p.m.

Well, I've calmed down a bit. Please excuse my temporary insanity! I don't know what is wrong with me lately. All I feel like doing is painting, listening to music, and trying to clean my room. Oh well. Death and dying, hating, crying.

I am so pissed!!! My mother and her friends are all sitting in the kitchen looking at pictures of me when I was little, when I had brown hair, and they're like, "She looked so much better!" I really hate that! It's so rude and it makes me want to cry!!! It's times like these that makes me want to tell them all to go to HELL.

⟿⟿

I think I'm going to give blood. Maybe I'll feel good about myself. Maybe I'm just going to give blood to get that little drop of blood pin. Who knows? The girl sitting next to me feels that you're giving part of your soul and spirit when you give blood. Hmmm…maybe I won't give. She's talking about how much the Red Cross charges people who need blood. A lot, I guess. I could go to the plasma donor place and get $10 for one pint. Whatever. I am going to give blood. It gives me a strange feeling when I think about it. I mean, I'll be watching my blood fill up. They're going to prick my finger. What if I have AIDS or something? It's scary. I hope I don't pass out. I'm paranoid, aren't I?

Well, I just called my pen pal in Cleveland. I guess we're going to stay at her parents' house the night of your show. I'm not quite sure if I'll be able to handle it. Their house is just about the dirtiest place I've ever been in. It's truly disgusting. I went to visit her last August. I got there on a Saturday and there was an opened mayonnaise jar on the dining room table. I left the following Thursday and it was still there! It looked as if they hadn't dusted in 10 years. I refused to eat anything. Anyway, we're going to stay there because it's free. In Columbus, we might sneak into this guy Seth's dorm.

Remember that heavy metal guy I wrote about? He's a devil worshiper. I found out today. Is the way you pronounce your name Nivek (Ny-vick) or Nivek (Nee-vek)? If I meet you and I pronounce it wrong I'll be really embarrassed. On MTV they pronounced it "Ny-vick" whatever. Do you like The Damned? I haven't listened to them in a long time. They remind me of John. Maybe I'll listen to them. I'm going to attempt to clean my room. I still wish I could be perfect.

⟿⟿

There's a place we must explore, open wide the door
—The Damned

I said before that I hated pain, but once when my mother hit me with a hanger, I didn't even care. It didn't even hurt. It was almost as if I blocked it. Confused? So am I.

Today I was telling my art teacher that I wished I were better in art class and guess what he said? "You don't realize how good you could be." That made me feel so good. I wish I could just stop thinking about it. I just know I'm setting myself up for a big fall.

I have a headache. Last summer I thought I had a tumor. How embarrassing, I almost fell backwards in my chair.

Guess what? Remember that heavy metal guy who I said was a devil worshiper? Well, I heard a rumor about that and I wasn't actually positive that it was true. Anyway, today he started talking to me and he said that he thought that I was into witchcraft. He was really surprised that I'm not. He told me that he is. I asked him if he is into devil worshiping and he said, "No, white magic." He said that black magic has to do with Satan. He handed me this book and told me to look at it. It's called *The Magic Power of Witchcraft.* I was kind of interested. It tells you how you can get in touch with the dead. Who knows for sure? I might read it. He practically demanded that I borrow it. Scary. He's paying so much attention to me. Why? Because I wear black? He has the neatest (such a large vocabulary I have) ring. It's the grim reaper. Whatever, I really don't want to get into witchcraft. I'm sure I could get into it. The problem is that I'd probably take it too far.

1 May 1987

Male Nurse: You look sickly pale.
Jolene: Thank you.
Male Nurse: You're taking that as a compliment?
Jolene: Yes.
Male Nurse: Oh, alright, but sit down before you pass out.

Yes, I've given blood. It didn't hurt. I thought it would. My blood is soooo dark. Get this, they give you this "personal" paper that asks you if you have ever been with a homosexual, a prostitute, etc. I almost fainted. This stupid guy keeps staring at me. It's so obvious. I mean, if he thinks I'm weird why doesn't he just come out and tell me instead of making me feel like I'm in some kind of freak show? He's truly strange.

11 May 1987

I'm about ready to take a Government test. I'm not too confident. I mean, I hardly studied. I suppose I'm relying on my cheerful attitude toward my teacher to pass. I am awfully nice and pleasant to him.

14 May 1987
12:12 a.m. (Journal)

I'm so infatuated with Nivek Ogre that it hurts! Well, I'm really nervous about the show this weekend.

16 May 1987
12:24 a.m. (Journal)

I'm so nervous I can barely stand it. I'm depressed. I should be excited. I've imagined every possible thing that could go wrong. I'm afraid that Nivek will forget to put me on the guest list. I really hope he hasn't forgotten. I'm so obsessed with him.

Scared. Depressed. I need to rest. It's actually today! Not even a whole 24 hours! I'm nervous. I'm not even ready.

✦

17 May 1987 (Journal)

I met Nivek Ogre! He's so sweet!

Matt and I got to Detroit at about 9. I got in with a fake ID. We got right up front and I talked to some girl from Canada. The opening act came on. By the time Skinny Puppy came on I was right against the stage. First I saw cEvin Key come out, then I saw Dwayne. The music started and then I could see Ogre behind this screen. You could see his silhouette. It had blood on it. He was holding a puppet that looked like a skeleton holding a cross with long claws. It was great. He came out and was wearing black pants and a white T-shirt. He had blood and mud all over him. He also had on broken black plastic glasses.

He looked at me and Matt said it seemed like he recognized me. He stood in front of me once and all of these people were crowding over me trying to touch him. I didn't. Their stage show was so excellent. So morbid. On the screens, they showed great scenes from movies. He had this wild mannequin torso with the stomach cut out. During "Dig It" he went behind the screen and it looked like he was pulling his intestines out.

After the show, I asked a roadie if he was with Skinny Puppy and he said that he was. I asked him if there was any way that I could get in touch with Ogre. I explained to him that Ogre wrote to me. He told me that he would speak to Steven Montgomery and explain the situation.

I looked up and saw Dwayne, cEvin and Ogre going up the stairs. I almost said Ni-vek. Then I almost said Ny-vek then I said "Kevin," and he turned around and put his finger up like "Wait a minute."

After a while, the other guy came down and said, "All right." So Beth and I went into this big room and I saw cEvin Key way in the back and as soon as I walked in Ogre said, "Jolene Siana." It was great. The first time I heard his real voice was when he said my name. He came over to me and said something about me being a "crazy kid," then he said that my letters are fascinating and very creative. He said that they get letters all the time and they are all the same, but that mine were different and that's why he wrote to me. He also said, "You really have it up here", as he pointed to his head, then said, "Don't ever lose it up here." I smiled. He said to "keep 'em coming," referring to the letters. Then he said, "So what's going on in your life?" We just stood there talking and then we walked over to this table where there was a whole bunch of food. He got me a beer, opened it, and then offered Beth one.

Dwayne was sitting by the window with some girl. Ogre came back to me and asked me how I liked the show. I said I thought it was great, but he said he didn't think so. He said it was better last night in Chicago. I mentioned going to Cleveland. He said that he had to go take a shower, but that he'd put me on the guest list +1 for Cleveland and give me a backstage pass and talk to me more. I was so excited. I ran downstairs and told Matt what happened. I looked in the mirror and my hair was flat.

I got a ride home with Beth and these 3 guys from Dayton. I was so hyper. I called Lindy when I got home. I got to sleep at about 4 a.m. I was awake at 7:45. We left for Cleveland at about 11. We got to Cleveland at about 2 p.m., earlier maybe. We went shopping at Coventry with Christy and Betsy. We went back to their house to get ready, then went to Peabody's. We hung out until about 8 p.m.

When the doors opened, I was not on the guest list. I was the first person in and I was so upset. I showed the security guard the letter that Ogre wrote me. The security guard took my letter upstairs, came back, and let me in. We got right up front and I saw this girl with a blonde mohawk. She was really happy because she had a backstage pass. I was upset. I went over to the security guard and I asked him if he could give Ogre the letter that I wrote him. He said he would so he went upstairs, then came back down and said that he couldn't find Ogre so he gave it to the tour manager, who said he would talk to me about a backstage pass. I waited and waited, then I heard him say the show was about to start, so I just went back by the stage. I watched the show.

Ogre

After the show I walked over to security and they were letting people with backstage passes in. I saw this girl that I saw in Detroit. I said, "Are you Ogre's girlfriend?" She said, "No I'm just his friend." I told her that I saw her in Detroit and that Ogre forgot to put me on the list and also forgot a backstage pass. She said, "Oh, Jolene, he was talking about you earlier." She said that he felt bad because he forgot to put me on the list. She said she would take me upstairs. We walked through this big room and he was standing with the girl with a blonde mohawk. They were talking, then he looked at me and said, "I have to go talk to this girl over here, she looks pretty depressed."

He kept asking me what was wrong and I said, "Nothing." He said, "I can't help you if you don't tell me what's wrong." I kept saying, "Nothing." I asked him if he got my letter that day and he said that he did but he hadn't read it. I told him it was really long and I didn't even know why he'd want to read it. He said, "They're fascinating." I said, "They're just about me," and he said, "So, I love them. Would I say it if I didn't mean it?" I said, "I don't know." He said, "Do you think I'm silly?" and I said, "No, I'm silly." He said, "Why are you doing this to yourself?" Then someone told him that someone had stolen the baby and IV bag. He jumped up and left. The mohawk girl approached me and said, "Why are you so depressed?" "I guess it's my nature," I replied.

Ogre came back and sat on the other side of me. We talked for a while. He said he was upset because someone stole some equipment. He said that he always gets depressed when people steal his things, so he's a little paranoid of being around people he doesn't know because he's had a lot of things stolen, including a special ring.

Ogre was playing with my necklaces. The mohawk girl kept talking to me and Ogre walked away. They started kicking everyone out, and I wanted to say goodbye, but the girl from Detroit said that everyone had to leave but she would tell him goodbye for me.

We started driving and got lost in a really bad neighborhood. I turned around and finally got to Christy's. I told her that we were going straight through. We left Cleveland at 2 a.m.

18 May 1987 (Journal)

We got to Columbus at around 5 a.m. Crazy. I can't believe I did that. I called Seth and he told us to come to his dorm room. Diane was sleeping

in the back seat and wouldn't get up so we left her there with a note telling her which dorm room we were in. I slept for about an hour and then we got ready.

When the doors opened I was on the guest list but no word of backstage. You had to be 19 to be downstairs. I was extremely upset. I tried talking to various security guards. Nothing happened. I saw Diane. She had a fake ID. I was so pissed. I asked this guard if he could get Ogre for me. He said he had no idea where the band was. I just walked around alone for awhile.

The security guard that I had been talking to said, "Hey, that Ogre guy wants to talk to you." I almost died. I stood outside and Ogre came out. I forget what he said but he was wearing the little blood drop pin that I gave him. I touched it. He was saying that he couldn't do anything about me getting downstairs because I'm underage. He said that he also couldn't use the gun with blanks.

I was nervously playing with my hands and twisting my rings and he grabbed them. He said that he knows what I'm going through with my grandparents and my mother but that I shouldn't give up. He said that he's lost people that he's loved and that I should "just write things down, that's what I do." He told me to keep writing him letters and that he would write me back and be my friend.

I wish I could remember everything. He said he'd get me a backstage pass and that he would talk to me after the show. When he came back he said, "I'll get you a better one that's laminated with a chainsaw on the back so you can keep it close to your heart." He took my hand and kissed me. He told me not to cry. He also said that I scared him because I show so much emotion. I ran into the Newport flashing my backstage pass given to me personally from Ogre!

After the show, I went backstage and waited and waited. Ogre walked by and said, "Jolene, I'm in a bad state of mind right now. I'm in an argument with someone, so could you please bear with me?"

Finally he came back with the mohawk girl from Cleveland. He came over to me and said, "I'm sorry I didn't get a chance to talk to you." I said, "That's all right." He asked me if I was going to keep writing him letters and I said yes. The mohawk girl kept giving me dirty looks. I said, "I guess I better go." He took my hand and gave me a friendly goodbye kiss. What a sweetheart.

19 May 1987
Columbus, Ohio (Seth's dorm)

Nivek-Kevin,

Hello. It's 7:45 a.m. and I can't sleep. I'm so bothered and confused. This is so childish but for some reason I can't stop thinking about you. You were so nice to me. Like I said, after I received your letter, I lived only for these past three days. Now it's over and I feel so empty. I don't know why exactly. It seems as though this infatuation has gone a bit too far and I'm hurting myself. Your letter made me feel so special.

I don't know why I was crying to you and I don't even know what I'm trying to say in this letter. Maybe I'm saying that I've clung to you so much that I'm hurting. Nivek or Kevin, whichever you prefer. I feel like I've given part of myself away. I have. I wrote things that I'd write in my journal and I'm so afraid that it's useless to you. I'm afraid that you'll throw them away or something. I'm really hurt and I can't understand. I'm not sure what I expected.

I understand why you couldn't talk to me. I'm obviously obsessed and I simply hate the way I feel. Please don't think I'm being stupid. I should learn not to share so much about myself. It does me no good. I really appreciate the fact that

... don't know why
i was crying

you said you'd be my friend. I really need one. I'm so lost in every possible way.

Will I ever be normal? I can't see how you would possibly want to be my friend being that I'm obviously infatuated and obsessed with you. Do you still "feel that need" to talk to me? I suppose I didn't live up to your expectations. I'm sorry. Shit, why do I do this to myself? I can't quit writing to you because I feel more lost when I'm not writing to you.

Don't forget me, o.k.? How could you forget someone as mentally twisted as me? Tell me one thing though, why did you say that you were "infatuated mentally and physically?" What did you mean by that?

><

At times like this I want to cry
I want to kiss the world goodbye
I want to be in present tense
I want to put up no defense
I want to go where I belong
I want to go where nothing's wrong

—Jolene

><

I'm fat and ugly, aren't I? My mother always says that. She's given me quite a complex. It's only 9:20 a.m. It's so dark in here. I'm embarrassed, because last night I was just so overwhelmed that I cried. I tried doing it discreetly but the phone rang and Seth turned the light on. I'm sorry. I do cry. I'm embarrassed for crying to you because it was a stupid thing to do. Thank you for talking to me though. I felt much better. I've always wanted an older brother. When I was younger I wanted an older brother so that I could fight with him. Strange.

I suppose I'd better end this letter.

You'll be hearing from me.

Take care,

Love-your mentally twisted friend,

J

25 May 1987

Nivek,

I can't believe some of the things people say. Diane has gone and told everyone that I've slept with her boyfriend. That's funny because she doesn't even have a boyfriend, unless you want to consider that guy Jeff that she met in Columbus her boyfriend. She's the one who spent the night with him. Not me. I'm sure, I've just about had it with her lies. Attention, do you think that's all she wants?

I keep thinking about this conversation my friends had yesterday about sex and AIDS. It's weird because you (in general) could have AIDS for 5 years and not even know it. That's scary.

My mother came storming into my room asking me where her brush was. It wasn't even 7:30 a.m. I, of course, was sleeping. She kept screaming and yelling. She's mental. I'm glad I'll be gone when she gets home. I'm not sure if I'm going to

Nick - do you mind if i call you Kevin. i mean - i called you Kevin in person. well kind of strange using two names. I bought a mini-cassette recorder. get in a good mood spend money. Actually, spending money today did not put me in a good mood im sad. so do you still crack your knuckles. i hardly know anything about you. you know a lot about me + that's scary because i keep telling you things about myself. why were you so nice to me? who knows why im depressed today. i suppose im just lonely. i want to get out of toledo. i really hope my aunt is going to give me that money she promised me. can you belive im actually watching television. that's true depression. i don't know what you're thinking. smothered hope. depression. smothered hope. depression. sometimes i get so happy - then - i think about all the bad things + i get really upset. with iod. im all alone. all alone. all alone all alone all alone all alone all alone all alone all alone all alone all alone death that party tomorrow. Their last party wasn't so great. I was going out with John then. Who really cares? I didn't get any mail today. That's sad. I love mail. I'm bored.

I had another dream about you. You met my grandmother. You guys were on tour and you stayed at her house. You made me leave but (this is strange) you wanted this girl Jodi (whom I hardly know) to stay so you could talk to her. Oh wow. I just remembered that David Lee Roth was in that dream. I really dislike that pervert.

Do you like Kommunity FK? I'm really upset because I forgot to look for their album while I still had money. I'm sick of my name. Jolene. Did you know The Sisters of Mercy do a version of that song, "Jolene"? I have to have it. That's so cool. One of my favorite bands doing a song with a title that's my name! It doesn't make me like my name any better though. I'm really sick of being hated by my mother. It's not like I'm a problem child, or am I?

"Living through one's own dementia." I look really gross today, as I do every other day (lately, anyway).

Jolene

〜〜

How many times have you been in love? Me? I thought I was "in love" when I was a freshman, but I hardly think so now. That was Todd. Then, my sophomore year, I went out with this guy Erick who was just too nice. I told him that I loved him, but I didn't. Nothing too physical ever went on between us. I ended up hurting him. I feel bad about that now. In my junior year it was Will. I hate to admit it but I loved him. Yes, even enough to end my friendship with my best friend. He never claimed to love me then, but now when he calls, all he says is how much he loved me and that he still cares for me. What a joke. Then…my senior year. John. Yes, I'd call it love—a rather strange kind of love. Maybe not even love, but a strong feeling for him, a crying out for the need of him to love me. Every year, I end up with one "serious" boyfriend. John and I weren't really serious, but we were. It's hard to explain. He's the only ex-boyfriend that I'd consider going out with again. He's a user though. He'd probably use me again. Oh well.

Last night I had a dream that I tried to kill myself. It was strange. I was in a hospital. I couldn't write to you. Weird dream. Would you come to my funeral? I'd like to have a really cool funeral. My mother would probably dress me in pink and she'd have my hair dyed back to brown. I'd haunt her. She's just <u>waiting</u> for me to kill myself. I'm serious. Oh, I don't get a graduation party anymore. WHO CARES? Just throw your life away and you'll be happy. What is your natural hair color? You don't even care. I guess I <u>might</u> go to that party tonight with Kim and Dale. That would be fun. Annihilate. Annihilate. Annihilate. Annihilate. Annihilate. Wrecked. It's all over.

I wouldn't want to relive my life. I hope I don't have another life. I used to think that if you're good in this life, then in your next life you have more going for you. For example, say you're really ugly and poor but quite sincere, in your next life you'll be attractive and you'll have money, but in <u>that</u> life, if you abuse your privileges, then your next life won't be so good, etc. Get it? They're simple examples but you understand, don't you?

26 May 1987

Ogre,

I'm so embarrassed because I just remembered something that I wrote in letter #1 or #2. That's the problem with mailing things off right away. I always regret something.

Anyway, I'm sure you'd think I was a mental case even if I hadn't written that but still, I cringe at the thought. My mother's friend just sat here and talked about Neil Diamond for about 10 minutes. She's seen him 25 times all over the U.S. She wants me to go see him with her some time. Oh, I can imagine that. I suppose he has a nice voice.

I wish I could change the way I looked and acted when I met you. Scar. It leaves a scar. It left a scar. Whatever. I feel so stupid. I wish I could do it all over again. I apologize for being so strange, sensitive and insecure. Who am I? Why am I? Who am I? Why am I? Who am I? Why am I? Who am I? Yesterday's words are gone. Help. For what?

My favorite song by Skinny Puppy is "Glass Houses." Do you want to "make it big"? I mean really big? Well, you're pretty big right now. They actually sell your records at Woodville Mall. That's like the smallest mall around.

You're sensitive aren't you? You seem like a sincere person. It's really cool how you guys (cEvin Key and Dwayne) aren't secluded from your fans. It shows how human you are. I mean when bands stay distant from their fans, that's why the fans get so hyper when they see the band.

I can't wait until Thursday. I hope that Jonathon is there. All I ever do is write. All I ever do is write to you. No, that's not true. I do find time to write to my pen pals. I've lost count on how many I have. A lot.

I'm almost afraid that I won't be accepted to college. I'm not stupid (well?), but my grades aren't too great. Everyone is trying to get me to apologize to Lindy. I haven't done anything to her and I'm not about to apologize. After what she said, there's no way. I'm actually very close to hating Lindy. I cannot wait to get out of school, then I can see who I want to see when I want to see them. Am I becoming a people hater? I hope not. I don't want to hate people. I am so tired, but I feel like writing.

You know I bet Lindy is going to try to do something to hurt me. She knows that I write to you and that I tell you things that I don't tell her, so she'll probably write to you and tell you all kinds of lies. Perhaps some truths, just to hurt me.

Guess what? My mother is with me 100% about going to England. I'm going to get information today. I think I already told you. I wonder when you'll get all of my letters. I wonder if you'll read them.

Hey, I finally met a nice skinhead. His name is Cory. At the party the other night, he kept saying, "I need a girlfriend." That's really funny because Diane hung out with him after your show in Columbus and I guess he kept saying that. That's sad. He's a nice guy. Personally, I don't think he's my type—though he is nice and good-looking. He's really into Skinny Puppy.

I love babies. I don't want one right now but I love them. They're so cute. I have to go to work in 30 minutes and I'm not looking forward to it. I'm tired and I have to close.

12:16 a.m.

I really wish I could write to you at work because I love the things that I think of. I really have no idea why my thinking is more clear there. It's strange. A lot of positive thoughts went through my mind tonight. That's good. I'm thinking about getting another job so that I'll have plenty of money when (if) I go to Europe. I'm really excited about that. I set some goals for myself. I'm going to get myself out of this hole even if it kills me. Why were you so nice to me? It baffles me. Seriously, I didn't think you'd write back. I'm still embarrassed and I will continue to apologize.

Oh, you know how Diane is an airhead? First she kept calling cEvin Key, "Kevin Keys," then she seriously thought he went by "Seven Seas"! If you don't take her seriously she's fun.

You have a deep appreciation of the arts and music.

i will not play at tug o'war
id rather play at hug o'war
where everyone hugs
instead of tuss,
where everyone giggles
and rolls on the rug
where everyone kisses
And everyone grins,
and everyone cuddles,
and everyone wins
Shel Silverstein

I'm determined to be happy. You know you might have literally saved my life? I'm serious, because I had that urge to end it all a few weeks ago but I didn't because I wanted to meet you. Doesn't that make you feel good? I remember once, this girl Sherry thought that she was pregnant and she wanted to kill herself because her boyfriend was really cruel to her. So, I befriended her and helped her out and she was so thankful and she ended up not being pregnant and she thanked me for "saving her life." That made me feel good inside that I could actually do that. I do like being nice and I feel good today.

Good night. Be good (my grandpa used to always say that).

Jolene

29 May 1987

Ogre,

Hello. As I knew it would my writing to you has slowed down a bit. Not by much, but…

My trip to the art museum was interesting. There was this display by David Hockney. He's British. He does the neatest work. He takes pictures, a lot of pictures and puts them together. I can't really explain. It's really cool though.

I went to the library today and I got some books on depression and suicide. As I read through them I get scared, because I <u>sound</u> like a suicidal adolescent!

I could never kill myself, but I want to talk to someone who will give me advice. I had these books lying out and my mother yelled at me. I'm sure. I'm depressed and she yells.

10:15 p.m.

I'm in one of those moods again. I'm trying to lighten up though. I wanted to stay home tonight. I could've gone out. I still could go out. I just might go out. Earlier I went out with Diane and two high school sluts. All they talked about was getting laid. They screamed at every guy that we drove by. The other one insisted that I'm a "punk" and asked me why I don't do acid. I'm not a "punk" and I'm not stupid enough to take acid. All of my friends do. I just don't get into drugs. What about you?

30 May 1987

Ogre,

Guess what? Well, I make the envelopes that I send to you in my art class. Today, as I was making some, my teacher Mr. Ramanowicz said that I should start making envelopes as a business. I laughed but he was serious! I was really flattered. Oh, I just got back from the store. Have you any idea what kind of people hang out at 7-11 at midnight?

Hey cool. I got a letter from this journalist for *Melody Maker*, Frank Owen. That's really strange. I met him in Cleveland last summer at a concert. I wrote to him asking him about his job and how he got into it. I wrote him so long ago that I almost completely forgot. Anyway, he finally did reply! I love mail. I'm sure you know. I've achieved a lot through writing.

Very soon I get to see Mark (my 6-year-old cousin). I'm so happy. I love him. He's so sweet. I haven't seen him for about 4 months.

A year ago today was my high school prom. I went with Jon Stainbrook, got drunk, got sick! It was awful. I hated it. The postman just came pounding at my door demanding $0.18 for your letter. The trouble I go through for you. Only kidding. I enjoy it. I really do. You're like my hobby or something. That sounds strange.

31 May 1987
Sunday
10:46 p.m.

My eye itches really bad. I wish I hadn't made such a bad impression meeting you. I'm almost too depressed to write. That's amazing. I don't ever recall being too depressed to write.

I almost threw a whole bunch of old letters out today but I saved them instead. I can't seem to throw anything away. I have this thing about the past. I save everything. Perhaps that's why I keep journals. I like to remember everything.

I don't know if I can handle staying up for 2 more hours. I'm afraid of dying. I don't know where I'll go. I don't want to be reincarnated. It's scary. I wish I could tell you things that you'd really like to hear.

Oh, yesterday we moved everything out of my grandparent's house. Kind of depressing. What if someone kills me? I'd hate for someone to stab me. I hate being sensitive. This school year hasn't been all that bad. It's been quite good actually, but the letdowns are so shitty. It could be worse, I suppose.

Jon's band The Stain

1 June 1987

Ogre,

Hello. I'm doing all right. Despite my mother's constant bitching! I'm watching Carson. Hey, I was almost killed today. I almost ran into a semi-truck head-on! His fault. My friend Brandy started crying. Not even 10 minutes after that, I pulled out in front of a car. DOOMED! Scary. It's so hot! It got up to 91 degrees today. It feels like that now.

2 June 1987

When you smile I want to cry. I don't want to die of old age. It's sad. Everything is sad. I'm not really sad today though.

10:36 p.m.

I'm thinking about my grandparents.

I got a perm. I look Italian.

Bye. Please Write.

Jolene

Demented and Sad

P.S. In one more week I will be 18. Legal, as Mr. Smith says.

〜〜

6 June 1987

Ogre,

I got another letter from another girl I met at your show in Columbus (she's from Cleveland though). She invited me to come visit. Her name is Jen and she told me to tell you "Hi," so "Hi" from Jen.

I have to make 4 tapes for people tonight. I don't mind really. I've been so creative lately. Shit, we're out of toothpaste. What am I going to do?

Guess what Mr. Ramanowicz said today? I showed him envelope #8 and he loved it. He said that he really likes my latest ones. He said that it looks like I put more thought into them. You'll be pleased to know (maybe) that I've been a lot more confident (today anyway). My hair looks 100% better, plus I read a story called "The Beautiful People." I really liked it. It's a short story in a Twilight Zone book. Anyway, I'm going to try to stay in this delightful mood. It makes me want to make everyone happy. It makes me thankful for <u>everything</u>. I'm going to bed now. Who cares, right? I CARE!

10:04 p.m.

Guess who's happy? Me! I'm happy. Care to know why? Something unexpected happened again. Jonathon called me! Why? That's what I wondered. He wants me to help him with a special project. Art, of course. He couldn't explain it over the phone, so we're going to get together and he's going to show me. I'm really excited about it. If it weren't for you this wouldn't be happening. A year ago I was so infatuated with this guy. Last summer he used to work at this record store and I used to go in about once a week. If he was there I'd buy an album, because I thought he'd catch on if I didn't. Last fall we became acquaintances and really nothing more. I'm so satisfied being his friend.

It's just so strange that about a year ago I would've died for this opportunity. Perhaps living isn't so bad after all. I'm so happy, I hope I'm as artistic as Jon Stainbrook says I am. I was supposed to help Jonathon silkscreen a shirt for The Stain (Jon's band). It never happened though. Oh, he's also going to help me with my drawing. Aren't I lucky?

The new album by Christian Death is so great. Do you have it or have you heard it? I'm really embarrassed because Jonathon is very proper. He appears to be so intelligent and I feel… [never finished sentence]

Who cares? I don't. I don't like being happy anymore! Please call me, I need help. I need to talk to you! Phil called me sick and demented because I rubbed blood-red tempera paint on my hands. It was fun. I was trying to be like you. I liked it. You think I'm awful, stupid, and crazy don't you? Oh, I must not forget depressed. I like being depressed. It's so lonely. All by myself. I own nothing. No one. Nothing.

If I really had to die, I'd like you to kill me because, well, that would be my wish. Would you do that? You wouldn't, would you? You'd get in too much trouble. But, you see, I don't want to kill myself. You could sacrifice me during a show. People would think it was fake. It would be so morbid. People would love it. Will I go to Hell? Is there a Hell? My mother really gets on my nerves. Why do I almost never smile? Death. Death. Death. Death. Death. I want to die.

7 June 1987
Ogre,

I'm bored with living. It's so tedious, you know? I mean, sometimes I feel it's worth it, but lately, I've tried to be happy and it seems as though I'm making a fool out of myself. After thinking that I'm happy I get really depressed and I cry. You know how in that one suicide book it said that crying over simply nothing is a bad sign? I've been doing that a lot.

Today at work some guy was telling our manager that he had to attend his friend's wake. His <u>best</u> friend. It made me really sad because I could see in his eyes that he was trying to hide his true feelings, then I felt <u>really</u> bad because he looked at me and said, "Smile, you always look so sad." <u>He</u> was telling <u>me</u> to smile. Then a few minutes later I was cleaning off a table and I noticed a lady who appeared to

tired tired tired tired tired tired tired tired tired
tired tired tired tired tired tired tired tired tired
tired tired tired tired tired tired tired tired tired
tired tired tired tired tired tired tired tired
tired tired tired tired tired tired tired tired tired
tired tired tired tired tired tired tired tired tired
tired tired tired tired tired tired tired tired tired
tired tired tired tired tired tired tired tired tired
tired tired tired tired tired tired tired tired tired
tired tired tired tired tired tired tired tired tired
tired tired tired tired tired tired tired tired tired
tired tired tired tired tired tired tired tired tired
tired tired tired tired tired tired tired tired tired
tired tired tired tired tired tired tired tired tired
tired tired tired tired tired tired tired tired tired
tired tired tired tired tired tired tired tired tired
tired tired tired tired tired tired tired tired tired
tired tired tired tired tired tired tired tired tired
tired tired tired tired tired tired tired tired tired
tired tired tired tired tired tired tired tired tired
tired tired tired tired tired tired tired tired tired
tired tired tired tired tired tired tired tired tired
tired tired tired tired tired tired tired tired tired
tired tired tired tired tired tired tired tired tired
tired tired tired tired tired tired tired tired tired
tired tired tired tired tired tired tired tired tired
tired tired tired tired tired tired tired tired tired

of lining of lining of lining of lining of lining
of lining of lining of lining of lining of lining
of lining of lining of lining of lining of lining
of lining of lining of lining of lining of lining of lining
of lining of lining of lining of lining of lining of
lining of lining of lining of lining of lining of
lining of lining of lining of lining of lining of
lining of lining of lining of lining of lining of
lining of lining of lining of lining of lining of lining
of lining of lining of lining is of lining of lining
of lining of lining of lining of lining of lining
of lining of lining of lining of lining of lining
of lining of lining of lining of lining of lining of
lining of lining of lining of lining of lining of
lining of lining of lining of lining of lining
of lining of lining of lining of lining of lining of
lining of lining of lining of lining of lining of
lining of lining of lining of lining of firesome lining
of lining of lining of lining of lining of lining of lining
of lining of lining of lining of lining of lining of
lining of lining of lining of lining of lining of
lining of lining of lining of lining of lining of
lining of lining of lining of lining of lining
of lining of lining of lining of lining of lining of
lining of lining of lining of lining of lining of
lining of lining of lining of lining of lining of lining

be in her early 60's sitting by herself. I thought, "She must be a widow." That alone made me sad, but then it brought to mind my own grandparents, gone forever. Love is gone. Worthless. Done. Depression. I started crying there at Sister's Chicken. Not bawling of course. Just a mellow teary sadness.

Why have I been crying? My right eye is swollen. Ugly. Of course. I'd really like to see you again before I go though. Perhaps luck will come my way. Hopeless devotion. I feel like a little girl. I'm sad. I kind of like to be sad, but I'm positive that I can't handle an average life. I want to die a relatively young and painless death. I don't have the slightest idea as to how I'm going to make it painless. Any suggestions? Perhaps it will just happen, right? Soon. Help. Good night.

2:20 a.m.

Will has called, and he wants sex. No thanks. Not tonight. I'm having a fun time talking to him. What we had is over. Stupid. He can't seem to get the hint. Oh, he says that I have a really smooth sexy tempting voice on the telephone. He said, "Maybe you better not answer the phone." This is simply hilarious. Oh no, he's starting to breathe heavily. He's the one who likes pain. That always bothered me. What am I wearing? He's wondering. I wish he'd stop. He's trying really hard to turn me on and it's just not working. Now he's trying to get me jealous. If only you could hear this. Now he's telling me he has had steamy dreams about me lately. Oh, I want to hear them! Why am I talking to him? Everyone likes back massages. Do I like baby oil? Give me a break. Memories. It's never going to be the same. Give it up, Will. He wants to mud wrestle. He wants to know if I dream about sex. Finally, I got rid of him! It's 3:05 a.m.

❦

I'm very upset. You know that I have a lot of pen pals, right? Well, this girl from Royal Oak, Michigan wrote to me. It happens to be that she is some sort of Skinny Puppy fanatic. Since I was going to go shopping in Royal Oak, I thought I'd meet her. She lives nearby.

She noticed that I'm a naturally depressed person, and she said it's not good for me to be depressed because of Skinny Puppy. I told her that I was depressed long before I'd ever even heard of you. Perhaps she thought it was all an act.

You have practically nothing to do with my depression. If anything, you make me happier. She seems to think that my life revolves around Skinny Puppy. You do in a slight way. I mean, I write to you constantly, but I also have a life. If that's what you want to call it. Oh, and she calls you "Ogie." You could probably care less, so I should just shut up.

Teen's dramatic suicide shocks, puzzles Flint suburb

I wish so badly that I could explain my most confusing feelings for you. It's not like, "Oh, you're Kevin Ogilvie/Nivek Ogre from Skinny Puppy be my friend, be my lover etc." It's just that when I wrote to you for the first time I needed someone, though I wrote to you <u>not</u> expecting a response. When I received your letter I thought, "Wow, someone actually cares about my feelings." I was <u>amazed</u>. I wanted to meet you. Not just because you're in Skinny Puppy, but because that was so thoughtful of you to write to me. I think you're such a nice person. Why?

I want you to know that my thoughts about suicide are not because of a so-called "influence" from bands like yours or Bauhaus or whatever. I've been thinking about suicide since, I believe, January of 1986. Not a long time. I hadn't heard of Skinny Puppy until exactly a year after. Oh, that girl also yelled at me because I just started liking your music this year. I'm sorry but it's not my fault that I hadn't been exposed to Skinny Puppy earlier. Right. So, I'm a loser all the way around, even when it comes to writing to you. At this moment I don't want to die as badly as I wanted to the other day. I can't deal with these extreme mood swings. Ogre, do you know what's wrong with me? Am I unsaveable? Should I give up completely or should I try once more? I better go.

Take Care—Love (is a weapon),

Jolene

8 June 1987
2:49 p.m.

I have time to explain just why I have covered your envelope with baby pictures of myself. Well, I am fascinated with childhood. When I was a child I had no worries—no major cares about anything. Children just live, learn, look cute, eat,

sleep, make messes and experiment! I love children. I was a cute kid. That was then. I hope you're not getting sick of my letters. I imagine you are, though.

My teacher, Mr. Romanowicz, photocopied 2 envelopes that I made for you. He is giving me extra credit for <u>all</u> of them even though <u>you</u> already have them.

Someone is at my door and I'm terrified. They are holding their finger on the doorbell. Who could it be? Who is it and why won't they leave me alone? My phone is ringing and I'm not going to answer it.

⤙⤚

Like you really care. OK, I'm about to say something really stupid. You, to me, seem like a big brother and a best friend put together. Why? I shall try to explain. A big brother is what I've always wanted. Someone to admire, someone to give me advice. A best friend is someone whom I can tell anything, someone whom I have something in common with. Oh, forget it. I can't seem to explain. What good is my existence? I wish I felt better. My head feels like it could explode any minute. That would be interesting. I love old people. I wish I could adopt a grandparent.

⤙⤚

10 June 1987 (my 18th birthday)

What a pleasant way to start a day! I might have failed my American Government exam. If I don't graduate I'm going to die. My mother will kill me. If she doesn't, I'll do it myself! I'm serious. I'm so scared. I hope I passed. I didn't even study for my English exam! Wish me luck.

Born: 6.10.69—Died: 6.10.87. Well, I took my English exam. I hope I did all right. I have graduation rehearsal. I don't want to go, but it's "required." I have to go buy a graduation dress. I'll probably look gross in it.

Some guy just gave me 2 blood drop pins. I'm going to give you one. Have you lost the one I gave you so long ago? I lost the one that I had. They're easy to lose.

As much as I hate to admit it, I have suicide potential. I think I do and I'm just about ready to go through with it. I hate myself. No one cares. I just want to give up. Quit facing the embarrassment and die. Leave me alone and let me live (die and rest in peace). I hate myself. I want to die. Drugs, second best to death. I really could care less if I die in a car accident on the way to work. I just don't want to suffer. Maybe I'll go play in the street or dive off the bridge or stick my head in hot grease at work.

11 June 1987

Yay! I passed my American Government exam. I got a D! The cookies we made for Mr. Samples must have made an impact.

12 June 1987

Well, I graduated. No big deal. Kind of boring actually. I never used to think that taking drugs was all right, recently though, I believe it's all right. Whatever. So many smart people take drugs and it hasn't really affected them, so why not, you know? I suppose I'm fascinated by drugs at this time in my life. I can't explain.

Jonathon called me yesterday. I'm going over to his house on Sunday. I'm tired. Diane is nothing but a bitch lately. I almost called her a whore, but I thought I better not. I just gave myself away but who cares. If I fucked every guy that looked at me, I'd expect to be called a whore too.

The worst thing happened to me today. We had just gone to this record store, we were passing the University of Toledo, and my car stalled. We were dead center on a busy street! I was so embarrassed! Luckily, there was a gas station about 50 feet away! I better go.

Take care all right?

The confused one.

June 1987

Ogre,

You're reading a letter from one confused (legal) adult (mentally still a child). Anyway, let me tell you about it. I went over to Jonathon's today. He and Courtney broke up. He had a picture of her, which he had drawn, hanging on his wall with a funeral flag placed in between 2 torn pieces of it. We listened to some records, then we went into the living room to watch some movie. It was called *Black Sabbath*. Anyway, he came over, sat by me, and asked me if I thought I was good at anything. I said, "Artistically, or anything, period?" He said, "Anything." I said, "Not really." I told him what I tell you. I'm all right in some things, but I'm not good in anything.

He went on to tell me that in order to be good in anything, it has to begin in your heart. He went to sit on the other couch.

A while later he came over to me and knelt by my side. I forget exactly what he said—oh yes, he asked me why I always embarrass myself (constantly). He asked me WHY. I couldn't answer. I began to tell him about my neverending paranoia and he kissed me and I thought, "What the fuck." It was an extremely different experience. He's so beautiful. But I don't want to like him.

You must know that I, for some reason, have developed some strong feelings for you! It's not LUST or anything dirty like that. It's more like a desire for a special friendship. If only you'd write me back. You don't think I'm being too fanatical about writing you, do you? You are my friend, aren't you? I'm confused.

Jonathon and I are going to Detroit tomorrow.

All together I've got $1,630! I'm definitely going to Europe! Of course I will buy you a gift!

If I died, would you come to my funeral? I'm serious. If I were to die in a freak accident and had a friend send you an invitation would you come? Would you care?

27 June 1987

Ogre,

Yes, I'm still hanging out with Jonathon. He's still lovely. I haven't written you lately because I've been so busy. I have been thinking of you though. I'm not taking those pills anymore. They really fucked me up and I just can't handle that. For a while I felt really great, but artificial happiness is pure bullshit. Of course alcohol isn't all that bad. Jonathon bought me peach schnapps. My mother doesn't even mind me spending the night at his house. Isn't that crazy?

I hope there's not a point when you quit reading your fan mail. I don't consider my letters fan mail. I consider them cries for help and attention. What do you think?

Jonathon thinks I put myself down too much. I'm going to change myself for him. He doesn't like me being obsessed with death either.

3 July 1987

Why do I hate people? Could it be because they're insincere, stupid, money hungry, selfish, and boring?

I'm at work and of course I'm in a very hating mood! This music is driving me crazy! It's the elevator mix of a Phil Collins song. SCREAM! I've been rude to just about everyone tonight, but do I seem to care? NO!

"I bet you don't know there is ice all over the floor?!" I bet I do know and I bet I hope you fall and crack your stupid head open!!!

I can't laugh at life anymore! It's too hard! I don't take chemicals in anymore. I drink sometimes, but it's a long story and I'm too embarrassed to tell it! I'm tired and I want to end this shitty day.

Just tell me to shut up!

August 1987

Well, almost every other day I seriously contemplate suicide and I'm scaring myself to death. Fucking death. Death. What's the matter with me? I almost hate life. I'm scared, confused and plain fucking lost. Ugly.

ᴗ~ᴗ

Nivek,

Hell O. When I cut my arm for you, Joelle said that you wouldn't care. Did I tell you that? Smile. Are you smiling? I didn't think so.

All I do now is take speed and drink. That's all right isn't it? Today when I was at the supermarket, I heard a little boy ask his mother if "bastard" is a bad word. I almost laughed. When I was young, I asked my mother the same thing.

Death is cool when you think about your own, but when you think of someone else's it's depressing. Especially if you know them. Oh, I don't know. Would you be sad if I died? Actually I did die and I'm writing to you from HELL.

ᴗ~ᴗ

Isn't it weird when you look at people and think, "Wow, they have hearts and brains and lungs?" I know it's a strange thought, but it freaks me out.

ᴗ~ᴗ

KEVIN OGILVIE ONLY PLEASE
Ogre,

I almost killed myself.

I cut my wrists. I can't take this anymore.

I came home from school to find that my mother scattered my belongings in my room. Why? Because she's fucking sick! She went on about how I'm no good, stupid, etc., and that she wants me out. She started hitting me, so I came into my room and shut my door but she opened it and continued to hit me. I started to go crazy. She

Kevin Ogilvie / Skinny Puppy
Yo Nettwerk Productions
Box 330
1755 Robson St.
Vancouver, B.C.
V6G 1C9
Canada

SUICIDE . . . a word that strikes a host of emotions when heard.
Fear, confusion, guilt, and anger. It is particularly devastating when
suicide affects the life of a student. Why would a young person want
to kill himself/herself when they have their whole life to look forward
to? This is a question often asked, yet suicide is now the second lead-
ing cause of death among adolescents.

Girls attempt suicide 3 times more often than boys.

524 Garden Place
Toledo, Ohio
43605-USA

i get frightened
just like you
i get frightened
too.

left my room and I just started crying and I couldn't stop. I found my razor blades. I cut my wrist just enough for it to bleed. I couldn't stop crying. I wanted to be able to dig the blade into my arm, but I kept crying. I wanted to die so badly. I wanted to bleed. I was clenching my wrist with my other hand and I could see the blood gushing between my fingers. I hate it. I needed someone. I went to meet Jonathon, but I missed him so I walked around looking insane. I could smell the flowers at my funeral, but I couldn't see anyone. You think I'm joking, don't you? I bet you think I'm trying to be cool by thinking of death all of the time. You probably think I'm trying to mock you because I like to see my blood. This isn't a joke. I seriously want to die and it seems like no one cares. I want so desperately for someone to care. You, Jonathon, anyone. If you think I'm just trying to get you to write back by telling you about my attempt of suicide, you're mistaken. I need to let my feelings out. You're the one I'm telling. You're the one I trust. I just wish you cared. I really need to write to you.

J

I thought about it. If I tried and didn't go through with it, I'd look really stupid. I'm so alone and it's my only way out. I have to. Please tell me I'll feel better. No one will care. But why, why should I? I'm not the only one with problems. It's just my fucking life. I am no one. I don't exist. I am dead. I have no one to talk to. I'm too sensitive. Life is too hard for me. I can't cope. I don't want to go to hell. But if it doesn't exist, I'll be all right. I feel sorry for her. Grandma and Grandpa will greet me. I love them. I need a hug. Thoughts of death. He can't walk and I want to die. She can't see and I want to die. He can't hear and I want to die. She's a vegetable cause she tried to die. I'm cold. Everyone is so cold. It's just too hard. I'm so confused. I don't have access to a gun.

PLEASE READ
Ogre,

I am so confused. It's so strange. Nothing is the same anymore. Last year at this time I was relatively secure. I knew what to expect (kind of) for my senior year at high school. My grandmother was alive. I didn't have a job. I had the same old friends. Now I'm going to move out. I need a job. I don't live near my grandparents' house or where I grew up. It's hard to take. I'm so messed up. I don't know what to expect. I haven't anything to cling to. I'm so scared and worried. Have you ever felt that way? I realize it's just part of growing up. I'm just not sure if I'm ready. I'm so used to relying on other people; that's why I want to be a kid again. No worries. Why must I be so confused?

Ogre,

Why do I hate this world? Because people, innocent people, can't even live in peace. I'm sure. Nothing is fair. What's wrong with me? Why do I read the obituaries? Why must I feel sorry for these people? Is it good or bad?

I hate these moods. It's almost like I put myself down and I can't find anything good about myself. I think about all of the things that I regret and I get sick. I hate looking in the mirror. I'd really love to give you this letter in person but as doubtful and insecure as I am I'll probably have to end up mailing it. I'll live. Some 90-year-old man died Friday. He got caught in an elevator.

19 August 1987
Ogre,

Smiles. Have you ever thought about how precious smiles are? When I make someone smile it makes me smile because I think I have the power to make someone happy.

The other night Jonathon and I were at work and I was in a VERY bad mood and Jonathon kept going out of his way to make me laugh. I felt kind of special. I said, "You always make me laugh" and he said, "That's all right because you keep me smiling too." That was nice. I don't know what I'm trying to say. It just made me feel good.

23 August 1987
Ogre,

Hello, even though I'm busy, I'm still bored and quite depressed. Death is indeed sad for the living ones. I just can't seem to understand why I am living. Fuck love. Why do I tell you about myself? Who knows? I'm sure you don't care. I need a friend. Actually, I have a good friend. Jonathon is a great friend, but he doesn't know as much about me as you do. Big deal. I always cry. I can't help being sensitive. Any suggestions? Kill myself? Oh, that reminds me. I found some razor blades lying around the house.

Do you ever cry? You seem sweet and sensitive. Crying is painful.
Love,
Your favorite (or least favorite) oppressed little girl.

18 September 1987
Ogre,

Hello. It's exactly 6 a.m. I just got home from work. What a thrilling evening. Anyway, I always get really depressed at work.

There is this one old man who always comes through the drive-thru. He's so cute. The other night our manager decided to close 10 minutes earlier and that man

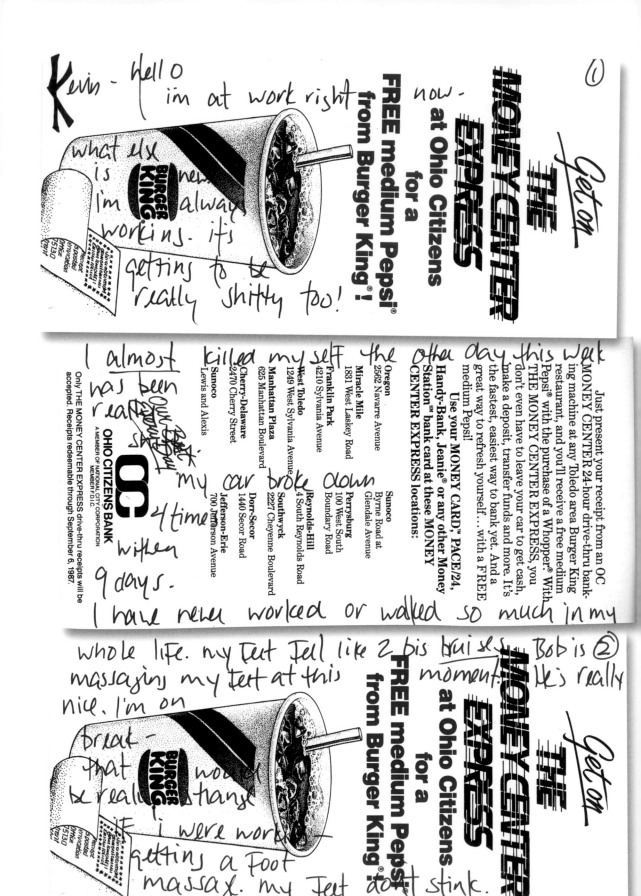

Handwritten (page ①):

Kevin - Hello   i'm at work right now -

what else is new   i'm always working. it's getting to be really shitty too!

Printed ad (middle strip):

Handwritten (middle strip):

the other day this week I almost killed my self   I almost was been really   our break everyday satuday   my car broke down   4 time within 9 days.

I have never worked or walked so much in my

Handwritten (page ②):

whole life. my feet feel like 2 big bruises. Bob is massaging my feet at this moment. He's really nice. I'm on break - that would be really strange if I were working getting a foot massage. my feet don't stink.

Anyway... i went into a drug store lookin for razor blades that i had been cryin so i didn't want to ask so i just looked all over the place. Hey - Bob just read my palm

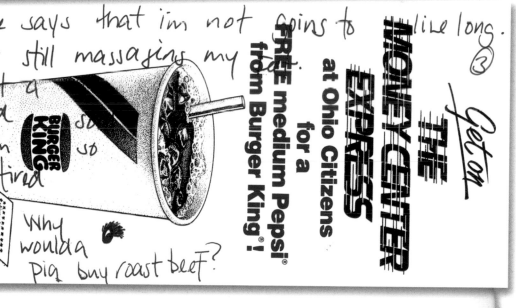

+ he says that im not goin to live long. He is still massaging my ... what a kind so so im tired

Why woulda pig buy roast beef?

pulled in and asked if we were closed. I was about to take his order, but my manager came over and told the man that we were closed. I was truly upset. I cling to familiar people because of my grandparents.

━━

Ogre,

I hate my mother so much. She is messing me up.

I'm not stupid.

I'm not ugly.

Why must she constantly nag? I'm lost. I'm addicted to writing to you. Something inside me thinks you just might care. It's possible. Perhaps.

━━

Ogre—as his friends call him…

I bought that *Star Hits* today. It cost $2.50, for just that one Skinny Puppy picture. I don't believe you're going to write me back. That thought puts me in a state of mild depression. There is always slight hope.

26 September 1987

Today is quite melancholy. Psychee called me. The cuts are still visible on my wrist. I'm going to get my picture taken so that you can see what I look like now.

October 1987

Ogre,

Please care about me. No one cares about me. She's sick and she's hurting me. I swear, I didn't do anything. I really don't want to kill myself, but I can't handle this. I want to talk to you or see you before I die. I cry all the time and I'm so worried. All I'm asking for is someone to care. Please.

━━

Have you ever been so depressed that you're absolutely nauseous at every single thought in your mind?

━━

Ogre,

I didn't write you last night because I was too depressed. I had another shitty day. I saw a movie on schizophrenia and it was scary. Some of my actions are on purpose, other actions I have no control over. I slit my wrist in my sleep. I cry.

My mother got up and she's nervously smoking her disgusting cigarette. I wasn't even going to watch this fucking special on the stock exchange, but I thought I would so I could learn something, but now she's up and I have to smell this disgusting smoke. I hate cigarettes. I hate life. I am really, really, really sick of life!

Go to hell. Get a life, people. I hate society. It's so fucking stupid. Oh no, depression. Fuck you. I've been depressed all my life. Can't you handle it?

~

Ogre,

Hi. What a day. I went out with my friend Kevin. I thought we'd argue but we got along nicely. He gave me his *Mind: The Perpetual Intercourse* tape even though I already have the record. Then he bought me all kinds of Halloween stuff. It was really crazy. We went to this place called the $1.98 store. It didn't kick in at first. Everything was $1.98. It was funny. Then we went to the mall and Kevin got on the computers at Radio Shack and I wrote "*Nivek Ogre is God*" and it said it all over the screen as it flashed. I wore a pink wig in this one store. It was fun.

~

Ogre,

Hi. Tonight was sort of cool. I went to the video store to get The Changing but I didn't see it. I did, however see The Tenant. I loved it. I watched it alone with the lights off except for the red light. Oh great, ex-boyfriend Will to interrupt the mood. It just figures. He's acting strangely, of course. Oh, he's sick but he wanted to call me. "I've been wanting to call you for so long." Oh, he's telling me I'm smart and he's glad I'm going to school. OK, Will, talk about our fucking past. As usual. Make me feel guilty. Talk. Apologize for calling so late when you always call me in the middle of the night. I'm so scared talking to him. It's really weird. He's talking about his waterbed. Oh, bad subject, Jolene. He says I sound more calmed down. All right. Whatever. He says I sound like I'm doing well. "I know this sounds stupid but I don't know, a lot of things remind me of you." Give me a break. You're truly nauseating me. Understand? "I talk to you about a lot of things that I don't ever talk about with other people."

October 1987

I'm scared because no one is mean to me at school. At first I thought those girls in my art class didn't like me, but they're all nice except for this one girl. She's not better than I am so I don't really care.

Anyway, people actually talk to me and that hasn't happened since junior year in high school. This good-looking alternative guy said hi to me like he knew me. I've never seen him before in my life. Strange. Maybe I'll see him tomorrow.

~

Hi. I'm at home. I hate work. I've been cutting my wrist a lot lately. No big deal. It's quite noticeable.

22 October 1987
11:37 p.m.

Ogre,

Well, I'm not so well. Last night I killed an animal. A rat, I think. It could've been a cat and I don't want to think about it. I was introduced to a girl named Renee. Heather brought her over. She's very nice and she loves Skinny Puppy. She died when she saw my room. I really like being nice to people, don't you? Of course you do. I hate rude and obnoxious people. I like being nice to people that deserve kindness.

28 October 1987

Today is hellish. The cuts become bigger each day. Deeper actually.

30 October 1987

Last night was so crazy. I went to a party with my friend Jackie. She's friends with my (and her) ex-boyfriend John. He's incredibly hot. Anyway, we went over to his house and I was so afraid he'd be mean to me.

I walked in last and he just looked at me as I stood at the door. I thought he was going to slam the door on me, but instead he said, "Oh, it's Jolene," and I was happy. Everyone there said I look really different. Jackie and I went out to the car to get her purse. When we walked back in I fell down the stairs. Along with my scream you could hear me fall. I was sitting there with my legs out and I was laughing so hard and so was everyone else. John smiled.

Before we left John said, "Oh, my brother said he meant to say hi to you but he didn't recognize you." When we left I said, "Why does everyone keep saying I look so different?" and Jackie, whom I haven't seen since the first week in September said, "Well, you look a lot prettier." I was like, "Oh, thank you!"

~~

31 October 1987

I can't concentrate. I'm thinking about—forget it. I'm just crazy. It's making me angry! I never ever want to. I'm so fucking sick of it all. I swear. I'm positive I get on your nerves. I'm truly sorry! I get so confused I go crazy and I can't stop writing. I promise I'll be normal someday. So fucking fanatical. I need a good cry. But the last special hug I had was from Milo and that was last July. The one before that was from my grandma. I wish I could hug you.

*Note: I think my mother read this. I left it out all night.

~~

Ogre,

Hello. I feel badly about wanting to die, because so many people have died who didn't want to die. I'm not sure if I can go through with it. I have a strong feeling already. If there is a hell that's where I'll go and I'm not sure I'm ready for hell.

17 November 1987

Yes Ogre, it's another letter to tell you how miserable my life is. But it is. I registered for winter classes. I don't know why I bothered. There's a 50% chance that I won't even live to go through with it. Leave me alone. You think I'm kidding about suicide, don't you? Well, I'm not. I lose a part of my mind each day. Depressing, isn't it?

Are you ever going to write me? I didn't think so. Have I written anything that has offended you? Hell on earth. Cry. Baby. Crybaby.

~~

I got splattered with grease yesterday. I was at work. Terry called me a "pretty girl" and said that he misses me working the late night shift. Oh, I guess I'm exotic, too! I'm sad, are you? Of course you are. Would you like any fries or anything

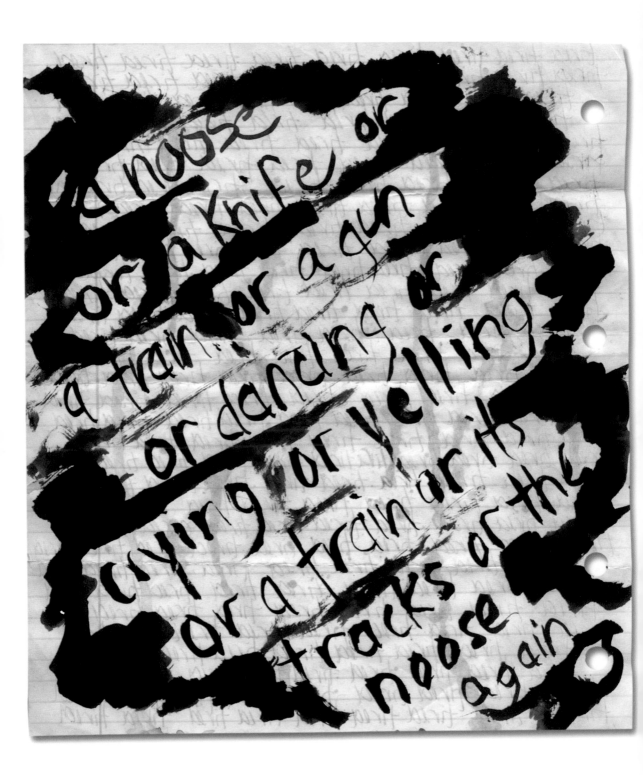

or anything that you think will work—as long as you die in the process it just doesn't matter

When: December 5th 1987 ad.
Where: 2550 Greenway Apt #11 bloodroom
time: 11:00 p.m.
rsvp: 535-9___ area code (919)

Please come ~~~~~~

yours,
JOLENE

im dying to see!

your presence
is most wanted
at this lovely

Suicide
Bloodfestival

to drink tonight? Oh, I get it. Tell me how do I feel? Tell me now, how do I feel? I feel suicidal because Benji isn't here and I don't feel love. What shall we do? They don't care and why else would/should I feel suicidal? Can you hold on—I have to go take some drugs.

5 December 1987

Ogre,

I'm at work right now and I'm depressed because I think no one likes me. Oh, Happy Birthday. I have to go now.

Well, it's the evening now. I'm a person! I called Nettwerk because I want to order T-shirts and I spoke to George. He asked my name and I said, "Jolene" and he said, "Oh, Jolene!" and I said, "What, you know me?" and yay! He said, "Yes, Ogre reads your letters all the time!" I felt so good. I'm smiling.

My stupid manager bitched me out today. He hurt my feelings and I cried. They don't like me there. I'm sure of it! But you still read my letters so my life is complete!

Love the red,
Jolene

6 December 1987

Oh, Ogre,

I fucked up! Danielle and I studied all fucking night! No sleep at all. She took Nuprin instead of NoDoze! Hilarious. Laugh. Then at Big Boy some foreigners tried to pick us up. Then Danielle forgot her keys, then we went to school, then we <u>FLUNKED</u>!

Yesterday my boss yelled at me because of my bad attitude. FUCK OFF.
Write soon,
Jolene
I'm still happy.

12 December 1987

Ogre,

No more drive-thru burgers. No more double Whoppers with cheese. I'm quitting Burger King. I got a job at the mall near my house. I will be working at a deli. I won't have to wear that hideous uniform anymore. Cool. I finally finished that abstract Skinny Puppy art piece for the show at school. I can't wait to give it to you. I really hope you like it. I spent a lot of time on it. I like the way I interpreted you.

Another day fucking life. Another fucking $100 for my car. My friend stuck her hand in a fry vat.

I'm such a loser. All I want to do anymore is write to you and sleep. I AM BORING.

The tape I'm sending you has some beautiful <u>material</u> on it. My grandma, grandpa, aunt, uncle, cousin, and my mother. It makes me cry whenever I hear it. Understand. I hope you listen to it. <u>Please</u> listen to it. It's very personal.

My grandmother used to sing to me when I would spend the night. We taped that December 25, 1983. Hey, isn't that when you started Skinny Puppy? This tape is quite the compilation tape. I hope you find it interesting.

꙰

Ogre,

Lobotomies are sad. Jack be nimble. Jack be quick. You're just so…You're just so… Don't play stupid.

Anyway, I get sick of girls and guys running around thinking they look so hot in their University of Toledo fraternity and sorority sweatshirts. I thought "Psychotic State" fit. It's cool. It fits my state.

Oh, my mother called your music devil music. Oh and I'm a "Satan Kid." Should I take it as a compliment or go commit suicide? She's watching the "Smothered Hope" video with me. Fuck off and die, bitch. I like her reaction: "Don't you dare show those videos to Mark and Brian." Well, isn't that sweet—she said, "I wish you were dead" to me.

I worked today. My new job is great. I just stand around and it's not stressful during rushes. I have a childish crush on a perfectly normal guy named Richie. The pervie Doug insisted that he was a male stripper. Ha.

13 December 1987

Kind of melancholy. Why haven't you written, dear? Do you think I'm Satan? You're just a person, why don't you write me? Ogre, you know I hate rejection. Please write. I'm CONVINCED you hate me. My life isn't complete. Make me laugh. Make me cry. Make me look all over the house for something to write on. Tell everyone in Toledo to fuck off except for me but I <u>refuse</u> to commit suicide.

Write me.

Scream garbled.

Help, I'm accident prone.

December 14, 1987

Ogre,

I'm trying to go to sleep but I can't. I can't.

Do I ever make you laugh?

Do I ever make you cry?

Do I ever make you sad?

Do I ever make you mad?

Do I ever make you think?

Wonder?

Solemn ponder?

Wander shake?

Why don't you care?

You say I show so much emotion. Am I interesting? Stupid? Young? Is my window open? Is someone going to kill me? Will I smile when/if I see you again? I'm not going to kill myself. Good night.

Love,

Jolene

Think of me when you tie your shoes.

15 December 1987

It used to be so easy to make people happy! Now all I do is bring people down. Why do I have to be this way? What happened? Yes, raindrops keep falling on my head! Fuck, I'm a loser. I might as well quit college. I have no idea what I want in life anyway.

I don't want to be a failure. I hate it. I hate being a failure. You're lucky—at least you're not a fuck up. You're doing something. You're making a living. Me? I have no future. I'll never make it as an artist. I'll never make it as a journalist. I'm lost! I'm <u>fucked!</u> Crying doesn't help. Nothing helps. You told me to write things down. It doesn't fucking help! I just end up looking like a messed up little girl to you. Why can't anyone help? Why won't people listen? Am I insane beyond repair or what? What the fuck did I do? My existence is bad. Bad luck. I should be dead or something. No, I'm not going to kill myself. I'm just in need of a friend or something.

⌇

Let's have a pillow fight. Well, today was quite full. Quite strange. I had to be to work at 1 p.m. I was tired and my manager was the usual rude asshole.

My ex-boyfriend John and his metal and skater friends came to the deli. I freaked and I was really nervous. John's friend ordered a pizza bagel, then John ordered a bagel with cream cheese. Pepperoni was flying all over the place. Then I gave John his bagel. He was very polite and I smiled.

Isn't it strange? It's like you used to be so close to somebody and then you feel so strange. I was in love with the guy. I was so nervous. What does that mean? And yes, I think he still feels something strange for me, too. It's very hard to explain. I feel badly. After he hurt me so badly I kind of got him back and I feel bad about it. Fuck. I regret it. He was just starting to go out with this girl and he told me to call him because he found out that I made out with his friend Todd. He was jealous. I was like, "Why should I call you? You're not better than Todd." I regret it.

I came home tonight and my mother said, "I hate you." What did I do, Ogre? Where did my dream boy go? He never existed, yet I am so in love with him. Do you know him? Does he really exist somewhere? Will I ever meet him? Can you help me find him?

What in the fuck did I do wrong? My mother just threw some Christmas presents that are supposed to be mine on the floor. What did I do? I wish you'd write me! I'm pathetic and that's why won't you write to me. You don't want to be a part of my pathetic little life! I have a bad stomachache. You know the kind of stomachache you get when you're feeling suicidal?

23 December 1987
Hi Ogre,

Darby

I'm in Flushing, Michigan, at my cousins' house. I'm watching Letterman. How are you? What are you doing? I'm wearing my "Psychotic State" T-shirt. I'm sitting with Kelly, the golden retriever. I let the puppy in. It's <u>soooo</u> cute. Its name is Darby.

I hate to admit it, but I think I'm infatuated with David Letterman. Only kidding. Or am I? I'm getting tired.

I think about it. I wonder, was I an abused child? True, my mother used to (and sometimes still does) hit me, but more than physically, she mentally and verbally abuses me. It hurts.

25 December 1987
Christmas
My mom stayed at my aunt's house for Christmas while everyone else (including me) went to my uncle's parents. They're really rich and conservative. Mrs. S. was talking down about some "queer" guy down the street, which offended me. I in turn, somehow managed to offend them by taking a midday nap and wearing my leather jacket all day long. So what. It was cold. They think I'm weird. Who cares?

28 December 1987

I didn't go to work today. I called in sick. I am sick. Mentally and physically. But I do know that I care. Do you? I'm tired and I'm not feeling well.

Love,

Jolene

Sweet dreams.

~~

29 December 1987

Ogre—

<u>A day in the life of Jolene</u>

Morning (dew). Mary Mae (mother of the insane) throws an AT&T phone at sleeping Jolene as "You stupid little bitch" is recorded into the little girl's nightmare. Jolene awakes at 11:50 a.m. Time to get up, tired one. She does a few dishes. Expecting a friend, are you? She writes a letter to a friend. Yes, Jolene got mail today from Scratch and Penny.

~~

My "mother" just went crazy. She's throwing things in my room. She ripped my posters and then she pulled my hair. <u>THIS IS NOT A JOKE</u>!!!!

A note to my mother:

You don't even care! You don't even care! Don't you understand?

When a person threatens to take their own life more than once a day, it is usually serious.

Don't you understand that I am sad and each time you blow off my threats, it hurts more and more? I am no one. I go to school, I work, and I cry. I am so sick of life and absolutely NO ONE cares! Why won't anyone care if I die? I'm not that bad, am I?

31 December 1987

Ogre,

Happy '88. I can't write to you anymore because it hurts too bad and all I ever do is think about writing to you and it hurts. It's silly, it's callow, it's nothing to you.

I can't think about anything without wanting to write to you. It's hard to explain. Please write anyway. It's been since May that I've been writing. I haven't wasted time, have I? Am I ignorant? Annoying? Don't lie. I'm annoying. I can't help it. It's so hard to change. I hate life.

Hi, I'm in Detroit at St. Andrews Hall. It's 10:45 p.m. We were supposed to go to Cleveland but we ended up in Detroit spending $12 to see 3 local bands. With $12 I could buy 4 cool pairs of earrings.

Why do people celebrate a new year anyway?

My last written words will be to you. I seem to have forgotten that you have a life. It won't be long. 2 minutes. Happy New Year. Oh, hugs and fucking kisses.

I can't write to you anymore because my friends told me not to. They say I speak too much of you. They just say it might be a good idea if I quit. I can't explain to them. I don't have to listen to them anyway. I love to write you, but you don't write back and I wonder if you hate me or something. I want to go to a psychiatrist, but I can't afford it.

As of now I have no desire to do away with myself. I'd just like to be myself without feeling so bad about it. I'd like to cry a little less. I'd like to be someone else actually. I want to be free but I'm so trapped inside myself. If I could understand my emotions, I wouldn't be so psycho.

I hope you'll be my friend when you tour. I hope you play "Glass Houses." I hope you remember me. I won't cry. I promise. I'll never stop caring about anything, because caring is so very important to me. Time is also important and precious.

I really don't know you and I'm sad about that. But I promise. I promise to be happier and more confident about whatever. I can't prove anything to myself.

So much I wish I could tell you. So many tears. Maybe you'll wonder how I'm doing or something. Maybe I won't be the inferior person anymore. Not the little girl. Well, thank you for your time. I sincerely mean it, because I've been told that I'm sincere. Take care of yourself because people really care. Love yourself. Don't hate me.

Jolene
Never forgotten.

Did I ever make you smile?

END 1987
Thank the Lord!

to: KEVIN OGILVIE (in a sane state of r
c/o NETTWERK PRODUCTIONS
BOX 330
755 ROBSON STREET
VANCOUVER, BRITISH COLUMBIA
V6G 1C9
CANADA

It's
My Life...
But your
Welcomed
To Have

by
Jolene Y

this is For Kevin
my reason
to live.
jolENE

Olo Network Productions
Box 330
1755 Robson Street
Vancouver, B.C.
V6G 1C9
CANADA

passages from the life of:

jolENE
2550 Greenway
Apartment # 11
toledo, ohio 43607-1380
usa

Donald Brown 1969-1986

If only we could turn back time
To ease a person's sorrow;
Would that enable us to change
One thing about tomorrow?

If only we knew how that night
Would change the lives of those
Who cared for him — But how could
we
See things God only knows?

If only we could stop the scourge
Of drugs across our land,
And give him one more chance because
He did not understand

The consequences of that night;
The pain his family bears,
The thought that's troubling all his
friends:
"If only I'd been there."

There are so many 'ifs' in life;
Too many 'ifs . . . although —
There is one more to add: Oh, Don,
If only you'd said, "No."

very sad.

*Heartbreaking.
If only he had realized
that things get better.*

January 1988

I take a lot of things for granted.

I can hear.

I can see.

I can walk.

I can write!

I can read!

I can run.

I can jump.

I have hair.

I don't have a bad complexion.

I'm not a street person.

I have a job.

I met you.

I should start being more thankful. Sometimes I think death would be so great, but then I feel so guilty for thinking that way.

1 January 1988 (I hate eights)

Ogre,

I've come up with a brilliant idea. I'm going to start writing to you only in this journal booklet. I thought that maybe if I did it this way, that you might possibly keep it. I've almost given up hope that you'll write back. It's kind of depressing but...I certainly can't dwell on it. Sad. I really have a bruise on my foot.

Love,

Jolene

Love-candles-blood-razor blades-nail polish-me!

4:02 a.m.

NERVOUS

I've been nervous before. Sometimes when I'm nervous, I laugh. Sometimes when I'm nervous, I shake. Sometimes I cry because I wonder why I'm so nervous. Sometimes I get so nervous I can be talked into almost anything. Once when I was nervous, I cut my wrists. It was different. It was for attention. Once when I was nervous, I cried in front of you. Once when I was nervous, I talked really fast and no one could understand what I was saying. Nerves are interesting, but I don't like being nervous. Nervousness almost caused me to give up.

DEATH

I'm not afraid of dying, I'm just afraid of how I will die. The kind, the ways of death. I'm terrified of being murdered. I have a fear that when I'm driving, if I pass a car the people in the car are going to shoot me in the head. I don't want anyone to slice my body up. I'm afraid of being stabbed to death. I don't want my body thrown in a river or put into a trunk of a car. I have a fear of having my head cut off. I don't want anyone to cut off my fingers and make me eat them. I don't want anyone to rip out my eyes with a fishhook. I don't want my skull crushed with anything. Not a car, a truck, a sledgehammer. Not anything! I don't want anyone to eat my nose. I have a fear of hot grease. I don't want anyone to stick my hand in a hot fry vat. I don't want anyone to hang me by my feet. I don't want to be nailed to a cross. I don't want anyone to pull all of my teeth out. I don't want to be in an airplane crash. I don't want to drown. I don't want to get AIDS. I don't want to go into a coma. I don't want to have an abortion. I don't want to fall down stairs face first. I don't want an animal to eat me. Shark, bear, lion, tiger, whale, cat, dog, anything. I don't want to catch on fire. I don't want to be buried alive. I don't want you to choke me. I don't want to be hit by a train. I don't know. I don't want my body parts scattered. I don't want to be scalped. I don't want fire in my eyes. After I'm dead it won't matter. I don't want to suffer. I want you to be there. I don't want to be alone. I want to die smiling. I want to see my grandparents. I don't want to go crazy. I don't want to be forgotten.

REGRETS

When I was at Girl Scout camp, I lied a lot. I said I had two sisters and then I pointed them out. I said I was older than I was. I stole three stamps. I threw some girl's toothbrush away. I got into another girl's mail. I was in third grade, eight years old.

I regret writing the mean letter to Grandpa.
I regret anything having to do with Will. Anything and everything. Age 16.
I regret going out with Jonathon instead of going to Detroit with The Descendents.

FRIENDS

I have friends, but no one knows everything about me. You know just about everything about me except for two things that I could never tell you. Beth is a good friend. I can trust her. I don't know. Lindy is sincere and she understands. Jonathon is a user and sometimes I <u>really</u> despise him. Psychee understands me. Blah. Blah. You don't care anyway.

LIKES

Writing. Black. Red. Blue. Green. Walking. Darkness. Cemeteries. Candles. Incense. Thinking. Sleeping. Dreaming. Laughing. Long hair. Old movies. Clothes. Hearing. Figuring. Traveling. Shopping. Letting out anger. Old things. New things. Being understood. Old people. Babies. Slow music. Depressing music (to help me understand that I'm not the only depressed person in this world). Crying when I need to. Writing you. Being alone. Talking on the phone long distance. Being told that I'm cared for. Compliments. You. Feeling safe. Crosses. Jewelry. Big watches. Getting my point across. Lyrics. Staying up all night. Driving alone on an empty road. Being scared, but knowing I'm safe. Church bells. The smell of churches. Halloween. Christmas. The smell of scotch tape. Saving money.

DISLIKES

Users. Being sick. Being made fun of. Being called stupid. Being tired and thirsty. Thinking about my grandparents' death. Sluts. Liars. The sun in my eyes. Suntans. Losing things. Messy rooms. Crying. Headaches. Sadness. Rejection. Pain. Studying. People in general. The radio. Trendy people. Boredom. Shallowness. Driving when I'm sleepy. Myself, sometimes. My mother, sometimes. George Michael. Whitney Houston. Sneezing. Sore throats. Cracking gum. Being left alone when I want in. Being used. Pepsi. People suffering. Hospitals. Running out of gas in a bad neighborhood.

The room was spinning
I grabbed the gun
Now let me see how this
is done.
If I pull the trigger my
Life will be through
Blood on the walls
What would you do?
—Jolene

QUESTIONER: Why did you kill your daughter, Ms. Siana?

MS. SIANA: I didn't.

QUESTIONER: You were the person seen coming out of the apartment after the shot was heard.

MS. SIANA: I said I didn't kill her.

QUESTIONER: Who did?

MS. SIANA: She killed herself.

No, she didn't.

2 January 1988

Today was the—oh, I won't say it. First my stupid car needed gas. I went to the bank machine and put my card in and the computer thing said, "We are retaining your card. Contact Toledo Trust." I was quite upset. Driving on fumes, I got to the mall to go to work and there were absolutely no fucking parking spaces. I saw this woman walking to her car, so I figured I could wait. So, I waited and waited and waited and I'm thinking, "What the fuck is that woman doing?" and then I noticed her stuffing her face. I waited 10 minutes. She still wasn't done pigging out so I drove around. I finally found one about 3 miles away.

After work, I went outside and looked all over hell for my car. When I finally spotted it, I slipped on the ice. Then my no-good car wouldn't start. Then, some guys were messing with me and I called home and no one answered! I let it ring like 34 times! So, this girl Jeanette gave me a ride home.

It's only the third day of 1988 and I'm getting close to the end. Well, I have a little way to go. This is strange, but I need you. I need you to read these letters. I need that. It's crazy, I know. But I'm addicted to writing you. I lied.

~✦

Oh to be the cream.
—Bauhaus

3 January 1988

Hi. Good Morning. I got up at 12:56. It's now 1:21 p.m. It's Saturday. Saturdays are so busy at work. I just know I'm going to be fired.

I feel bad, because I shouldn't think about death. It's such a confusing worry. Sometimes I could just kill myself and other times I wonder why I even thought that. Death is weird. People want to kill themselves and no one can stop them. Lindy's cousin worked in a mental hospital and even when they'd lock people in a room they'd try to do it by digging their fingers into their veins on their wrists. One lady got a hold of an eggshell and tried doing it that way. I could stick this felt tip pen into my wrist and keep stabbing it. You could do almost anything. Fishhooks scare me.

Mail Art
by Ayse°lo

What about knives, forks, needles, pens, exacto blades in your eyes? That's a scary thought.

Hmm…I wonder if I'll get any mail today. My poor little car is stranded in the Franklin Park Mall's parking lot. I hope no one breaks into it.

4 January 1988
10:31 a.m.

Why do people enjoy making me feel stupid? Lately I'm so nervous. No wonder I'm insecure. I'm no one. I can't relate with anyone. I hate everything about myself. It's so hard. Why does it have to be like this?

Oh, guess what? Our phone may be turned off tomorrow. I paid my mother $40. She's complaining because she thinks I owe her more. Watch, one of these days you'll feel like calling and my phone will be disconnected.

Hi Ogre,

I'm watching *Sesame Street*. My astronomy class was pretty cool. It's a large class— like 200 people! The professor is foreign. I think he's French but he speaks with a German accent. He discovered a comet. I have an art class at 6 p.m.

Art Class

I feel really stupid because I didn't bring any drawing supplies. Oh well. If he makes me look dumb, I'll look dumb. What's 5 more minutes of embarrassment in my life?

I really think I'm going to enjoy Astronomy. I've always been interested in planets and such. When I was younger I used to lie in bed and think, what if there were no planets, no people. <u>NOTHING</u>. I would try to picture just blackness and no one being there to see it.

These are words I like to say:

Persist, macabre, insidious, exasperating, invocation, function, bludgeoned, fixture, blood, demented, extraordinary, hospitalize, collision, melancholy, psychotic, Polanski, rigor mortis, insecure, sultry, ceasing, synagogue, Massachusetts, Gahan, necromancy, lament, obscure, etc.

I don't care if I'm here tomorrow...
—New Order

Well, I am officially a college student. It doesn't feel so different. I live right up the street from the University of Toledo. I can walk there and I do, most of the time. My classes seem cool–Design, Astronomy, Drawing, Public Speaking and Algebra. I will never love algebra.

12:04 a.m.

Why do I write about myself? Do I confuse you? Is there any effect at all? Do you really keep my letters? I bet I'm the youngest one in my art class.

I had a friend named Pippi who was bisexual. She was really nice. We were pen pals. She always talked about suicide and she liked pain. I haven't heard from her in a while. I hope she didn't kill herself. Do you pray? Do you sleep at night? Do you think I'm demented? Are my letters exasperating? If I was the only person alive on earth, I'd listen to music all of the time. I wouldn't be afraid to go to the cemetery at night (alone). I'd probably be lonely. I'd go into everyone's houses. I'd drive across the country. I'd be sad, I suppose.

No hearing, or breathing or moving. No lyrics. Just nothing.
—New Order

5 January 1988

Were you a spoiled child? Do you like yourself? You really should. Do you read the Bible? Is your hair still black? Mine goes to my shoulder blades in the back. You know, I hate to sound ungrateful but my mother bought me a lot of bright clothes. Needless to say they're going to be returned. I'm sure! White pants and a bright turquoise shirt. I'll pass. I'll return them to get my leather boots.

Your perpetual pest from Toledo.

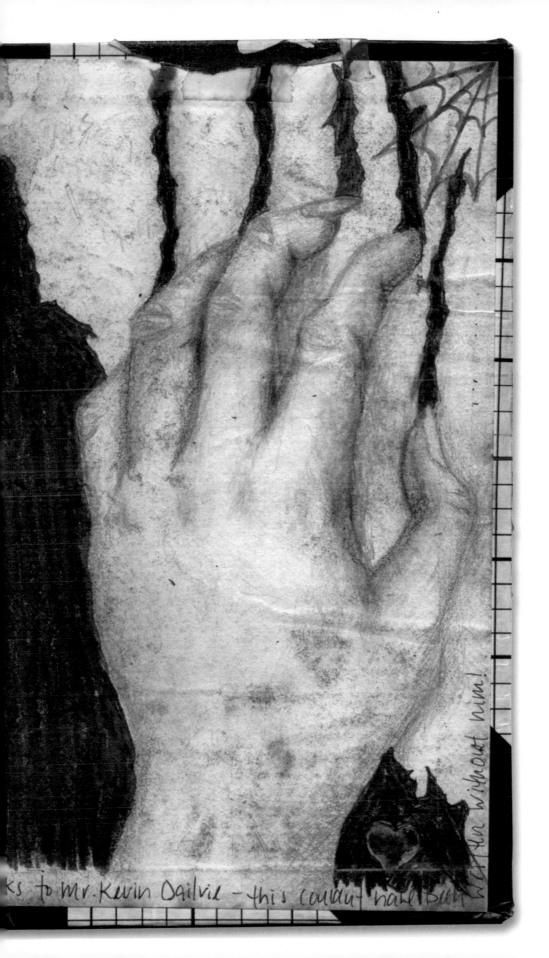

ks to mr. Kevin Ogilvie - this couldn't have been written without him!

73

11:01 p.m.

Hi. I should be doing my algebra homework but I'd rather write you. Don't worry. I'll finish it. My photography class should be pretty fun. My mother just came into my room and yelled at me. She said I'm slowly killing her and I said, "Good." It's so fucking cold in here! I really hate her. She said when the lease for this apartment is up she's going to move out. GOOD. She's a stupid bitch anyway. Why should I care? It's depressing knowing that I came out of her. She's such an alcoholic. Oh great. Now she's smoking. I hate the way she smokes. So nervously. Makes me want to throw this pencil at her. Maybe she'll go to bed now. Good. She's going to bed now. I think I might go to bed too.

6 January 1988

Oprah Winfrey is on. This guy is talking about his 12-year-old son who molested a 4-year-old girl. Oh, this is really sad. I remember that when I was about 4 years old, my mother's friend's son wanted to play "husband and wife." Then when I was in kindergarten, my babysitter's brother used to ask me all kinds of perverted questions.

This guy I knew raped this other guy's sister. He was 18 and the girl was only 10. She was really sweet. I met her before. The guy who did it was really psycho. He stabbed his girlfriend's father with a screwdriver. He always said he wouldn't live past 20, but I wonder. I wonder if he's alive. He could be in jail. He used to always give me back massages in class.

Have you ever done cocaine? Me? No, not that. I have to get ready for class in a few minutes.

8 January 1988

Hi, I'm Jolene and I have nothing better to do than write to you. Does that upset you or flatter you? Or, are you just neutral about the whole situation? What's a tear garden? I don't want to die. I've decided that. No, I'll live until I have to stop. I do have a fear of AIDS. Willies. Chills. Shingles. Popcorn. Yellow school buses. Nonsense.

Hello. I'm back. Working at Burger King was a waste of my life. What are you living for? Heart full of stone. I'm dumb, aren't I? I've always felt uncomfortable saying, "AREN'T"

BEAUTIFUL. Isn't it? You'd better say YES!

but I refuse to say "AIN'T" just because it sounds better. It's low-class and I hate low-class. I have a secret and I bet that I can keep it.

8 January 1988
10:20 a.m.

Death.

My mother pulled a knife on me.

Every time I look at her I wonder why she hates me, but then I look into the mirror and my question is answered. She hates me because I don't love myself and I don't love anyone and neither does she.

9 January 1988
3:01 a.m.

My depression is <u>not</u> caused by you. I get <u>SO</u> mad sometimes. Not like it matters or anything but I do get mad! Like <u>really</u> mad.

In the darkness
Where it's cold and muddy.
I would like to love somebody.

10 January 1988

I hate her more than anything! She wishes I would die and I hope for the same thing. You don't even care. NO ONE DOES. All right. On Christmas, when I was at my aunt and uncle's, I went to my aunt's parents'-in-law. My aunt told my mother that I kept my coat on all day and my mother said that everyone thinks I'm weird. The thing that really upsets me is that I have no one to turn to anymore. Not like friends but like parent figures. Tonight my aunt wasn't even on my side. I was so hurt. My aunt said that both my mother and I are SELFISH and I was crying and I said, "I'm sick of hearing about what's wrong with me." And she said, "You know we all love you." FUCK OFF!

11 January 1988
Ogre,

Hi. I'm at school and I don't remember where I put my book! If my mother finds it I know she'll look through it. This morning I got up at 6:30 a.m. It wasn't until about 6:45 that I remembered that I didn't have class until 9 a.m. So I kept resetting my alarm until 8:15, then my mother came in and started screaming. I got some of it on tape.

I don't have a family anymore. Now my aunt's house is off the list in case I HAVE to get away. I have to get my mother wishing DEATH for me on tape. Maybe then you'll see how serious I am! I guess I'll have to get married if I want a family, otherwise I'll die of loneliness. Will you be my big brother? Why can't I stop writing to you? I can't believe she said she was going to kill me. Has anyone ever said that to you? It hurt.

I have no one to parent me anymore. Everyone thinks I'm strange. So what if I am? Nothing can be done. It's over and I'm sad. I used to cry before my grandparents died. I cried because I didn't want to lose them and I cried when I lost them and I cry because no one else really gives a fuck.

10:20 a.m.

I need some speed. I want to run away. Even though suicide is a sick and demented word, I like it. I don't want to commit suicide, though, because I'd feel guilty. I could wait for my mother to kill me. What if it happened just like in my dream that night last year? I'm so tired. I'm sad and my insides don't feel well either. I can't help it. It wasn't my choice. They died and there went everything. All of this isn't supposed to be happening. I'm not supposed to be sad, cold, hurting forever. What will make me smile? Adopt a new family? Wasn't I a good kid? I sense a really fucked up adult life and it makes me angry! What did I do wrong? I can't understand. I know what I did wrong, but why did I do it? What do I look like in your mind? Am I a scattered mess? I'll have a nervous breakdown if you refuse to read these letters. Oh fuck! I'm getting upset. I just pictured myself taking a bunch of pills but instead of dying I messed up my brain and I still lived—in an eternal more insane HELL. Not only do I scare you but I scare myself as well. 18 years old. I hate it! Is it going to end before I'm 19?

12 January 1988

So, after algebra my friend and I were standing there talking outside of class, and I was holding my Roman Polanski book and she asked me about it and I said, "He's really cool but he's kind of strange. He had sex with a 12-year-old." Some guy passing by gave me a really strange look. It was hilarious. Then I was coming upstairs to my little private space and I ran into some guy head on. We both apologized and I continued to walk and he said, "Hey," and I turned around and he said, "You have pretty eyes," and I said, "Thank you." Bizarre?

Yesterday after school I was driving down my street and my mother had just pulled up and I was thinking, "Fuck, I have to spend the whole day with her!" but as I was walking up to the door my aunt pulled up. I was surprised because she lives two hours away. My aunt bought me my camera. A Pentax K-1000 and I also got my glasses. Don't laugh. I only need them for school, so there! Oh, you'll never believe this, but you know that attractive guy in my algebra class? Well, he has an accent! I think it's British! Isn't that cool? I die when I hear an accent.

Please please please let me get what I want this time.
—The Smiths

13 January 1988

I'm really excited about my photography class. I told Lindy that if I die to make sure you get this. See how important it is? I'm glad I don't have to work today. I can't wait to take pictures.

11:24 p.m.

Well, guess what I had to do in Drawing today? Yes, draw a nude woman. Of course I was uncomfortable. I didn't think that came until anatomy. I got 6 rolls of film today. Black and white. I can't wait to get started on my photos.

I remember when Karl from the Descendents wondered why I'm so depressed. He said he's into life and to not be sad. Then he and Milo asked me if I cut my wrists. I said no. I'd really like to hear from him. Well, I have to get some sleep. Love yourself.

Bye

Jolene Marie Siana

15 January 1988
8:12 a.m.

Suicide is murder.

Can't anyone just sit down with me and tell me how to be better? Are they giving you my letters or did they just lie? I'm so confused! If I ever understand my feelings it will be a miracle. No, I'm not getting mad at you. I really don't know you. You probably know me better than I know myself!

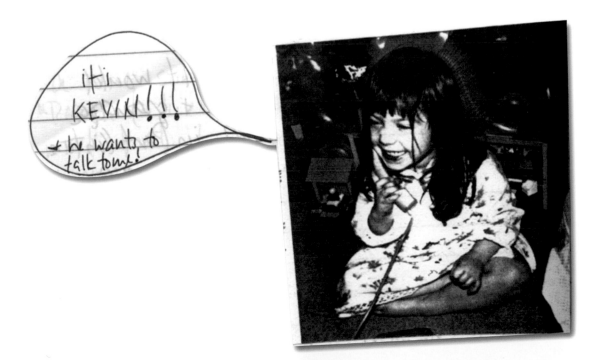

prettiest ink in the world

she took the blade and looked at you life isn't so bad, so they say - but for her- she had only you - and even though she really didn't know there was something about you, she thought. sincerity. but it ext went to what will? - I know that you understand what ired tr to say, this book means a lot to me. that is why i chose to write in blood for the final page. any pen doesn't agree with the blood. I you see the importance of this book that is why i cut myself just for you. sure it's been done before but th is is for you - espec For you. From me. It not something you can buy a shop it's mine and i have chosen you to keep it please. i will be upset if you throw it out or something. keep it and read it whenever. i think you'll write back because im not dead yet an when i do die you can remem mashin 419 535 9101 2950 greenwas #1 TOLEDO OHIO, 43 6017 1580 USA though it's not love it means something. Believe it

you will writ My anne.

She just said she's leaving. She said that I could decorate the house any way I want—like my "ugly room." I know she'll be back but honestly, I don't care! WELL…I think I'll be staying out all night! I have the option. Maybe I'll come visit you, wherever you are.

21 January 1988

Hi. It's the 21st. I got *Rosemary's Baby* and *Helter Skelter* on video.

As I was walking into a store, some stupid, low-class guy who was with another low-class guy and a low-class girl yelled, "Black is beautiful." Then he repeated it, then he said, "Tasty" three times and I looked up at him and he said, "You sure are beautiful." and I said, "GO TO HELL!" and he looked kind of scared or something but when I looked away he said, "I'll blow your fucking car up." So what?

Anyway, I'm still so depressed because of *Helter Skelter*. Those poor people. I feel really sorry for Roman. He's 55 now. I wish I could meet him. He has a movie coming out. It's so upsetting. It makes me want to cry. I've been depressed for two days. One and a half actually. I'm really tired.

8 February 1988

Ogre,

You may not consider me a friend or a part of your daily, weekly, monthly life, but please don't be depressed. I'm sorry that my letters aren't uplifting. I wish I could make you smile. Please be happy. I apologize for being so stupid. I'm not always depressed. Usually it's when I'm depressed that I write. That's why you don't hear much happiness from me. I wish I could tell you something funny. Do you ever watch Burns and Allen? Are you ticklish? Hey, I saw my heavy metal friend Jack the other day and he told me he bought *Cleanse, Fold and Manipulate* and he loves it. I said, "Cool!"

Be happy. Are you happy? It's gotta be good for you. Just tell me to shut up. Peace on Earth—it will never happen.

Jolene

~~

Hello. Well, I finished your book and I think this is my last letter to you. So, you will be touring Europe in April? Hopefully I'll hear from you before then.

BOOK TWO

March 1988

Hi. About the cover. It's great. Isn't it? Full of subliminal goodies. Guess who helped? Peter Murphy! No, I'm not big on autographs, but as you will find out later (the whole boring story) in the top left hand corner, he wrote "To Kevin, Peter Murphy" then he made a tear under the tear that I made on that sad  man. He liked my design. He thought I was giving it to Kevin Haskins. I said, "No, it's for my friend Kevin." Sorry I called you a friend. I had to. He complimented my artwork!!!!!!!

Ogre,

According to the Chinese zodiac you were born during the year of the tiger. I was born during the year of the rooster. Anyway, I'm going to write in here until you get back from Europe. Oh, boredom. When you're driving, do you ever get the urge to bash into the person in front of you? Me too. I don't wish to harm the person, just to get them out of the way. I'm so fucking bored. I'm so fucking bored. I'm so fucking bored. I'm so fucking bored. I'm so fucking bored.

My psychology book is totally cool. It has so much in it. Case studies on David Berkowitz, John Hinckley, Jr., and Charles Manson. There are a few sad pictures of monkeys though. They called Manson an "antisocial personality." I'm not social but I'm not going to send friends out to kill innocent people. Well, I guess I'll have to read about it. Jenny just asked if she could have a picture of me to paint from. She said I'm interesting. Dark hair, pale skin, red lipstick. Oh yes, I'm quite an original. Yes, that's sarcasm. I stole it.

4 March 1988

I was in a good mood yesterday and this girl Jeanie at work said, "You have such a cute personality, it's too bad you hate everything." I don't really hate <u>everything</u>. Anyway, Doug, the one guy that I work with has a big fat gut and he's always complaining about it but he eats all the time. He thinks he's hot and he thinks that I like him because I always tease him. I pinch his stomach and poke it with my finger like they do to the Pillsbury Doughboy in the television commercials. He told Jeanie that I can't keep my hands off of him and I'm like, "Oh yes, Doug. I just lust after you so badly that I have to just poke your stomach." Funny!

5 March 1988

Ogre,

Hello. Yesterday was hell. I worked and I came home with the worst headache I've ever had. It made me sick all over. It was awful. I felt like someone took my eyes and pushed them all the way back into my head. I couldn't get to sleep. I was in excruciating pain. I started crying and my mother woke up and started yelling at me for crying. She threatened to throw a glass at me. I'm sure, like it's my fault. Gee, I want to make my mom angry so I think I'll make myself have the worst headache in the history of my life!

Tiffany called and we talked about how great Roman Polanski is. Both of us like to think we're infatuated with him but really we're not. Guess what? I will finally admit that I have a slight crush on my drawing instructor. Next Wednesday I get to spend 20 minutes alone with him.

Why am I attracted to men who are old enough to be my father? Jon Stainbrook says that at a certain age girls subconsciously want to have sex with their fathers. Could it be because I don't have a father? I was born on a coconut tree. I'm scared. I'm getting my hair cut tomorrow.

8 March 1988

Ogre,

Hi. I don't know what a nervous breakdown is but I think I'm having one. Last night I was quite upset because of what's going on here. School, mother, etc. This morning I wanted to kill myself but I calmed down because I went to the cemetery and took pictures, then I went to work and I kept thinking that it's really no fair that I have to work every single weekend. I never have time for myself, it's such a nice day, etc. So, I changed and went into the deli. I put on my apron and I saw a notice

on the board for me: "Jolene: You have to help out instead of trying to get other people to do things for you. You also have to sweep and mop." That did it. I'm sick and tired of being picked on. I do my equal share. It's so fucked there. Nothing is organized. I just started shaking. I went way in the

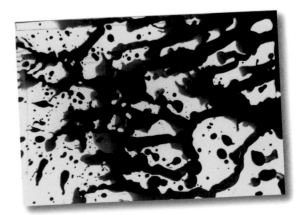

back and I just stood there and I started crying, then Jeanie came by and hit me with the door and I told Tina that I quit and I just left.

As I was walking down the hall they opened the door and said, "Jolene, are you coming back?" and I said, "No." Then I came home and did the dishes.

⤜⤛

Do you know how to have fun? Your song "Addiction" is so sad. I don't know why but I get so depressed. The lyrics and the way you sing it. Do you hate? Are you scary?

⤜⤛

Set me on fire, Kerosene
—Big Black

⤜⤛

25 March 1988
8:30 p.m.
Ogre,

I really can't stand it anymore. I was taping something off the television and my mother came in and threatened to kill me. She says I'm no good and she hates me. You don't know how much I hurt. I can't stand it. I can't stand crying. Then she was going to hit me with a coffee cup. I HATE living like this. What's wrong with me? I swear I'm going crazy. My brain is fucked. This world is fucked! I fucking quit.

I'm sorry, but what am I supposed to do? You know I don't want to die. I never used to like hate. It has overpowered me. I'm too weak to fight or care. I didn't plan it that way. Where can I go? I'm so sick of this. I honestly do try to smile.

Sweet dreams.

⤜⤛

27 March 1988
Sunday
11:00 a.m.

Chills. Chills. A woman was found chopped to pieces down by the Maumee River. Pieces. There is a psycho in Toledo. The weird thing about it is that I know who she was.

⤜⤛

Why can't I forget? I'm not so awful, am I? I feel like crying but not for me, for this fucking world. Why do people have to be murdered? Why do they have to die? I don't want to die. Suicide. Homicide. I don't want to die. I'm scared.

⤜⤛

Hi. Sadness. Disgustingness. Hopelessness. The killer of the woman in Toledo used to go to the beauty shop where my mom works, and his ex wife still does. Sick. Sick. Sick. It was the most gruesome murder in Toledo. It's so fucking demented. Murder. Death. I'm sick of the whole thing. Today has been really depressing. I hope I don't die in Detroit tomorrow. Love you. Hate you. There's lazy and there's rejection.

29 March 1988

Hi, I'm back. I have bad chills. That's so sad about that woman being murdered. I don't want to talk about it, but I do. I knew her. When we lived in an apartment on Main Street, she used to visit this woman Polly who lived downstairs. She was kind of odd. I felt sorry for her. She has a son who is my age. She used to, as Polly would say, "bum cigarettes" off Polly. My mother was annoyed by her. Maybe she thought she was better. I don't know. She was on welfare. Her whole life was just so sad. What a horrible, horrible ending.

It's just so pathetic. Those psychotic killers. It's awful and makes me even more PARANOID. Why life? Could it, oh, it's too sick to talk about. I have scars on my leg for you, dear. I cut myself for you. How pathetic. Who do I think you are?

I hope I don't get in an accident. I'm watching the movie *Manson*. It's interesting. Have you ever seen it? All those people could have had a good life.

Manson ordered the girls to have babies and they did and then they gave their children acid. The kids smoked pot and participated in orgies! That's so fucking pathetic. You should watch it.

My mother is making so much noise! I'm trying to watch this. Susan Atkins said the world is one big fuck. That is so disgusting I can't even write this. She sucked the blood from his mouth. They relate it all to sex. This is awful. I guess you have to see it. Never ask why. You know, Manson was born in Ohio.

All I do is write and write and write and get rid of bad feelings just like Ronny Moorings and you, too.

Hello,

I keep thinking about how strange my history professor is. He talks about how when he sees couples in public kissing he wonders how they have sex. Strange humans on a strange planet.

3 April 1988

Ogre,

Hi, it's Easter. Well, I'm just hanging out in my room while everyone is hanging out in the living room. My 17-year-old cousin is here and she came into my room for a while and said, "Skinny Puppy...I've heard of them." So I started showing her all of the concert pictures and then she said, "I'm going to the other room to see what those guys are doing." So here I am alone again. You know it's no surprise.

My mom's Easter Decor

My aunt from Michigan brought me some information on an art school in Detroit. I feel really dumb being in here all alone but you know how that goes. I'd really like to take a nap. My cousin Mark is so cute. It's so weird that my family doesn't really know me. Should I go into the other room and read to appear to be semi-social? No thanks. I'm all right in my room. Room. Living space. This is a waste of time. I love this song. You too? Oh, they're getting ready to eat. Please don't make me go out there, I hate out there.

18 April 1988

Lindy called. She and I talked about all the gross things we would do instead of kissing mean Seth. Some extremes were: kissing a cow on the mouth, kissing a pig, kissing a worm, risking death, kissing a centipede, eating a centipede and lastly, eating a cockroach.

I drove by my grade school and I saw my 4th grade teacher. She was cool. I was her pet. She always bought me things. She was pretty young. She related to me somehow, maybe because I was an only child and she was a widow. Her hair was black too. Once I organized a birthday party for her in our school gym. I also had one for my two 6th grade teachers.

Mrs. Rossler called me the "densest person" she ever met. Exact words. I was deeply hurt. She said it in front of the whole math class. What a bitch. Isn't it funny how you think of things that happened a long time ago and how they might

Here I am once again.
Once again fucked in the
head wondering why I
have to be me.
Anyone else but me.
I'm going to sleep huddled
up in the corner tonight.
Give mommy dearest
a scar.
My smile is ugly.
I am ugly. I'm sick in
the head + id love to drift
away. Picture a dead soul and
a zombie - that's me all right.
Fucking dead in the head. you and

have contributed to insecurity, paranoia, and self-criticism? I'd like to show that woman a few things now.

⟡

20 April 1988

Psychology is over. I have to go to World History because I skipped on Tuesday. I hate it. It hasn't even been half an hour. It feels like forever. I was born here. I've been listening to history all my life. Don't you hate when you look into someone's eyes and you can't look away? Not because you like them. You just catch their eyes and you stare and it's like you can't look away. That just happened. It happened with my history professor.

⟡

When the minutes drag...
—Love and Rockets

⟡

I'm going to see ALL in Detroit tonight. I asked my design teacher how he liked the tape that I made him and he said, "It's different." He called Skinny Puppy "a little bizarre." Then he mocked you. It was so funny.

I just picked Kristy up. The car is going to be full.

(On the way to Detroit)

I can't concentrate on one fucking thing. I have no idea what we're listening to. Not like it's bad or anything. It's just too fucking loud. I'm trying to think about how I'm going to decorate the cover of your book. My book. I love writing to you. I love most of the things I love only sometimes, but I love to write you all the time. Understand? It's getting dark. In case you didn't know I'm in a car right now. It's getting dark so I won't be writing for much longer.

I can't see what I'm writing now and I'm really annoyed because I can't hear. I can hear this fucking music. TOO LOUD. I should put my purse over the speakers. ANNOYING. Hear one R.E.M. song, you've heard them all! I'm going to have nightmares about too loud R.E.M.

We're at the club. Gooch just called me "Death Glam" and he called Brandy "Life Glam."

⟡

I do wonder what my father looks like. What if he's a murderer? I know he probably doesn't even know I exist. Some guys never know. This girl named Tina who I used to be pretty good friends with used to sleep around. In her junior year she got pregnant not even knowing who the father was. She kept the baby. That's strange. I wonder if my father would want to see me. Jenny and I are going to see Peter Murphy in Cincinnati. I hope Jenny gets an interview. I need another pep talk. Will you give me one? I have rights as a human being.

EMOTION CONFUSION OBSESSION

I wonder what my sister looks like. She's 2 years older than me. I wonder if she's as psychotic as I am. Maybe she's dead. Morbid thought. Sorry. You don't know for sure.

24 April 1988

Oh, today my mom told me that her friend Jan from work said that she should never complain about me because I'm so sweet! I guess she really likes me because I'm quiet and just sweet. My mom said that all of her friends were complimenting me…I do like compliments. Do you? I guess they really don't know that deep down inside I'm selfish and sometimes cruel.

I love old people and babies and when people are nice to me. Today I went to buy some tapes and this black lady was staring at me and I looked at her and she said, "You're dressed cute." And I said, "Thank you." I was shocked!

I want to be special. I want to be remembered. I'm strange looking. Am I strange looking? Do I have good insides? Please say I have good insides. I've been dead for twenty years. Is it a ghost? I pinched my arm.

Well, I went to the party. Weird. It was in a yucky neighborhood. It was small and packed and a band was playing. I mostly talked to Kristen. This guy who I've seen around a lot, a Sid Vicious look-alike, was carrying around a whisky bottle. He got right up in my face and offered me some. No thanks. Then later he was drinking and he said something like, "Here's to Waite High School," and I went to Waite, so I said, "Did you go to Waite?" and he said that he did and I said, "I went to Waite." He said, "I know."

I guess Shaun and Suzanne are getting a divorce. That's really sad, but I knew inside it couldn't last. Karen is way too intelligent. She's 25 and Shane is 20. He wrecked 3 cars. He was an alcoholic. He stopped drinking but he still smokes pot and does acid. Sad, sad life.

You still might think I'm the groupie type, but you must understand that I need a brother/friend. You don't owe me anything. You can be my brother in the Navy with no time to write. Yeah, that's it. Addiction is sad! It really is.

You know, I was thinking, people get so mad at me for being paranoid about death. One contributor may be that all the priests that would preach to us would say, "Don't ever leave your parents or people you love without telling them you love them, because they might die and you would feel guilty." The teachers would say that too. So you constantly think about your grandparents or mother not being alive when you go home from school. I remember crying about not wanting my grandparents to die.

26 April 1988

Ogre,

The woman in front of me is falling asleep. I hope she doesn't fall out of her seat. I wonder if she's under a great amount of stress right now.

Motion sickness. I have to tell you about the dream I had on Monday night. You know how I'm paranoid? Well, I keep having dreams about shootings. A whole bunch of people from my old high school and myself were in Chicago and I was paranoid about being shot. I kept looking for suspicious people. Then I saw this normal looking woman and I thought, she looks like a trustworthy person but you never know, then she pulled out a gun and shot randomly, everywhere. We found out that she killed someone that we were with and we were really upset. Luckily this person doesn't really exist in real life. Why do I have dreams about death all the time?

I don't know why I get so tired. I get enough sleep. What's my problem? Corruption. White, white skin. You know, I don't know about Beth in Arizona anymore. It makes me mad because she's always talking about how much money her father makes. Big deal. On Sunday, she kept talking about how good she looked and that she's beautiful.

7:15 p.m.

Are you going through a lot? Are people bothering you? Do you think you can stop them? Then why don't you stop them? <u>I'm worried about you</u>. I don't think you should kill yourself. It's just not wise. You know what I'm talking about. It's none of my business, but I don't know why. When was the last time you cried? We're all having strange dreams. You don't have to feel weird. You can if you want to.

READ!

When you are confused you remain confused because no one wants to spend their precious time explaining to you how things work and it gets so annoying and you get frustrated and you want to cry but no tears come out so all you do is pout and people get confused and they remain confused because you don't want to spend your precious time explaining to them how things work and they get so annoyed and they get so frustrated and they want to cry but no tears come out so all they do is pout and you ask why but it's so hard to explain and you are confused and you remain confused.

I saw the after-whatever of an accident today. Pretty bad. It could have been me. If I die, I don't want anyone reading my journals. I want them to be sent to you. They're too personal. They're embarrassing. Ugh, I have to wait an hour and ten minutes before I can go to the bathroom. I can't believe I write so much to you. Please don't throw them out!

Some asshole man in California or somewhere raped a 15-year-old then cut off her arms with an axe! He's out! And this man said that he's worried about his own life because he's received death threats! Fuckhead.

28 April 1988

Hi. You know I never really took time to study the lyrics of *Cleanse, Fold and Manipulate* until today. Well, I know "First Aid," "Addiction," "Deep Down Trauma Hounds," and "Anger," but what is "Mourn" about? I wish I could write like you. You'll go down in history. I just don't like the cover. I don't know why. It's just not like the rest.

The Peter Murphy show is on Friday. I guess I'm driving. Watch, my car will break down. I asked Annie to come along. My letters to you are esoteric. I've added a word to my vocabulary.

That is life. It symbolizes life because, well, the bottom part is the past, which is dark and all pushed together. It branches out on the present. The present that I have interpreted is spread out and symbolizes your thoughts in general. You have more control over your present than your past. In your present you may be preparing for the future, but the future (to the right) is clear. Blank. Because it hasn't been touched yet. But, as you can see in my design, everything you do affects your future. It's all linked together. The past, the present, and the future. I called it life because it is life the way I see it in my mind.

Jolene

＊＊

I went to look for a job. I bought Peter Murphy's album. I'm so glad the lyrics are in it. It's such a pretty song, "My Last Two Weeks." I went to Woolworth's to apply and this girl told me to ask "the woman in red and green" if they were hiring and so I did and the old woman said, "Don't ask me, honey, you have to go all the way back there," and I was like, FUCK YOU OLD WOMAN! I refrained. Anyway, I hate looking for a job. I think I'll skip history class.

＊＊

I said I'd write a letter but I never got the time.
—Depeche Mode

＊＊

I feel really embarrassed because someone just called and said, "Is this the lady of the house?" and I said, "No, she's in the bathtub," and he said, "Is your dad there?" and I said, "No," and he said, "When is a good time to call back?" and I said, "I don't know, a couple of hours," and he said, "That's a long bath." Funny. It was someone from the Police Department.

4 May 1988
12:03 p.m.

Hi again. I'm going to Cincinnati tomorrow. I hope that I don't die.

＊＊

Dear Mr. Ogre,

Hi. Weird mood. I saw Peter Murphy last night. We interviewed Passion Fodder, then talked to Peter Murphy. I had my design with me because I was going to work on it while they were interviewing. I had Peter write hi. He liked it. I was flattered that Peter Murphy liked my artwork. Wouldn't you be flattered? You probably know him anyway. He was really nice at first, but then he was, like, really distant.

When we were waiting outside I met these two guys who are really into Skinny Puppy and we talked. One said that he and his friend went on your bus last May and he called you guys major druggies because whatever, nothing important. But he knows you're really intelligent.

I'm kind of upset with Annie. She called me a bastard child because my mother wasn't married. She wasn't talking about me at first. She said people who aren't married and have babies have bastard children! I took much offense, wouldn't you?

I find myself maturing each day. I blame my insanity phase on a slight case of dementia praecox. It's 12:30 a.m. and I have the urge to clean my room.

it breaks my heart to
tell you this but
last night they played
smothered hope
        + - sit
        ready
    There were
    $ let it
    be a nightmare!
    TRENDIES
        dancing to
        it. I hope
            youre
        not taking it
        badly.
    "i think im   I thought
    pregnant"   you should
                        know.

    Don't worry -
    perhaps they'll
    go out + buy your
    records + you'll make   lots of
    money.

92

Ogre,

I got an apology from Annie in the mail today. She apologized for half a page for calling me a bastard and she sent me a picture of you backstage. I smile.

Where do my dreams go when I'm awake? People who have narcolepsy fall right into REM sleep, skipping all other stages of sleep. They start dreaming. They fall into a dream. Are dreams going on somewhere in my brain when I'm awake? I have to know.

I just wish and keep on wishing. If someone would die for you, would you change? The truth? Slit wrists or sleeping pills. Would it get better? Don't look so morose. What a fool I've made out of myself.

I don't have a crush on my psychology professor because he was annoyed at my class today and I didn't do anything wrong. That's why. If you don't want me to have a crush on you, don't be mean to me because I don't have a crush on you. I just told you. I like your brain. It's hardly a crush. I just want to be your friend. Remember that. I can be sweet. Well, it may give you chills but I'm a little bit fascinated by your personality. Understand? I wonder what it's like to be tall. Want to trade places for a day? Actually you live my life each time you read a letter from me.

Well, it's nice to know I'm not the only one who doesn't get anything out of his lectures. My professor is old and he has this macho tan. I bet he's like Roman Polanski. I bet he still has sex. You know, you can just tell. Some old men are grandpa cute and some have that arrogant look which I don't find attractive at all. I mean, Roman Polanski is different because he looks younger than he is, but this professor of mine is not young-looking.

I'll tell you about that ALL show that I meant to tell you about so very long ago. It was in the worst part of Detroit. These hip-hop guys and one teenage girl kept trying to get into the show for free. Well, towards the end the girl at the entrance gave up and let them in. At first they were laughing at everyone, especially the guys who were slamming. They started slamming as a joke and this one skinhead almost started a fight.

They were right up by the band. I was kind of scared. Amy was kind of scared too. Later we found out that everyone in the band (except for Bill the drummer, of course) was scared. When ALL was done with their set, those guys took the microphone and Stephen (the guitarist) jumped on drums and started a beat and Karl played bass and those guys started rapping and making all of these dumb noises and the lights that had been on for the whole show were turned on and off and off and on like disco-style, you know, and everyone started dancing. It was so hilarious. Then when they were done they said, "That be ALL." It was just too funny. I guess you had to be there.

━━⟋⟋━━

Everyone makes mistakes, oh yes they do.
Big people.
Small people.
Matter of fact, all people.
Everyone makes mistakes, so why can't you?
—Big Bird

━━⟋⟋━━

Guess what? I called George at Nettwerk. I asked if he received my last letter and he said, "Yes, you're really funny, Jolene," and I said, "Really, why?" and he said, "You're fucking hilarious," and I was like, "What are you talking about?" and he said, "There was glitter on the floor for like 5 days. Your name came up at least once a day." I put A LOT of glitter in my letter.

━━⟋⟋━━

I can have my own opinion when I write. I can say whatever I want to, even if the person that I'm writing to disagrees with what I'm writing. I can write it anyway. I can write and write and write to you and even if you never write back, I'll keep writing to you because I need to. Emptiness. My mom said, "It's over!" once again. Once again, it's over.

━━⟋⟋━━

Hello, I just got into an argument with Lindy. I went all the way over to her house because we were going to rent a movie. Anyway, I was playing the interview with you that Psychee sent me and I made her listen to the whole thing before she got out of the car, and when it was done she said, quite sarcastically, "That's the mind of a genius," and I said, "You really don't need to put him down," and she said, "You don't have to get so defensive. You don't even know him," and I said, "I know him better than you know Morrissey," because she's writing to him.

6 May 1988

Hi. It's tomorrow. I love my cute typewriter. Guess what else George says? He asked me when was the last time I talked to you. I said, " You mean that the last time I actually spoke to him?" and I muffled, "Almost a year ago. " And he said, "What? " So I repeated myself and he said, "Oh, that's not good," and I said, "I know," and he said, "Well, he knows you're around," and I said, "I know that." Then there was silence. Whatever that means.

11 May 1988

Ogre,

Hi, I'm at the museum. I'm really sick of everything. Tans are really pathetic. I went to the Toledo Zoo today with Jenny and my mother. I saw one of the pandas. I saw a baby gorilla. I'm getting nauseous thinking about all of this writing going to waste. I know I annoy you and I feel bad about that. Sorry. I apologize. Smash frat houses. And sorority houses too.

11:30 p.m.

I will be 19 in 19 days! Oh, did I tell you I got a job? I'll be a cashier at Hill's Department Store. It's like a K-Mart. BLAH. I'm tired of wasting time. Class was boring this evening. We talked about Freud again and I hope you don't know much about him because his weird stories include a definition of paranoia, which is a fear of homosexuality. No, that's not a fear of mine.

I bought my Revolting Cocks ticket, but I may not have a ride. I got another part-time job at K-Mart in the shoe department. Jenny got it for me. I bought some cool nylons. Jackie, my friend who had a baby, called and wanted to do something. Having a baby or something changed her. She lays out in the sun. She loves baby books and she talks about the past a lot.

12 May 1988

Just a little demented letter to say hello. See, I was going to do a design for you in my beautiful blood, but it keeps clotting, so I quit. I hope you enjoy my book when you get it. The picture on the front of the envelope is from my kindergarten year. The principal, Sister Mary Ellen, thought I was the cutest kindergartner so she made me act like I was talking to her and get my picture taken. So shy was I, and still am.

My heart bleeds and I feel as if I am on drugs but in reality I am high on my delusions. I'll be 19 soon. I can buy liquor in Canada.

Perpetual pest. Jolene

For you
a devotion so pathetic and
painfully true from this silent
soul.

this is me
dripping a positive
for you.
KEVIN

may you always
remember

to: Kevin Ogilvie
c/o Nettwerk Productions
Box 330
1755 Robson st.
Vancouver, BC
V6G 3B7
CANADA

& then
grew up.
☹

SISTER · TAKES TIME TO LISTEN.

From cute little John

to: Kevin Ogilvie c/o Nettwerk
Box 330
1755 Robson St
Vancouver, BC V6G-3B7
CANADA

The Art Institute of Pittsburgh called me today. I bet you really care. Jenny stuck an orange down her pants and she said it's making her horny. She's truly sick and quite perverted.

Hello. I'm dumb. I skipped my History exam! Bad. Stupid kid.

There's kerosene around.
Probably come to die in this town.
Live here my whole life.
Never anything to do in this town.
Live here my whole life.
Stare at each other,
Wait till we DIE
There's kerosene around-
Something to do.
SET ME ON FIRE.
KEROSENE
—Big Black

16 May 1988
12:59 a.m.

One whole demented partially lonely year. Anyway, you know how I don't consider myself Catholic anymore? Well I'm kind of upset with the Catholic Church. I mean, why should I have to tell all of my "SINS" to anyone? O.K., so I believe in God. What difference does it make if I tell God my sins through praying rather than going to a priest and confessing to him? I don't understand. Why must I tell a priest? What does he do, tell God himself? When I had my first confession, I was supposed to feel cleansed or something. I didn't. Actually, I felt BAD because I was too embarrassed to tell the priest everything. Well, thanks for letting me share that with you. I confess to you as I told you once before.

18 May 1988
12:49 a.m.

I went to my grandparents' graves yesterday. I can't drop my history class unless I talk to my professor and let him take care of it.

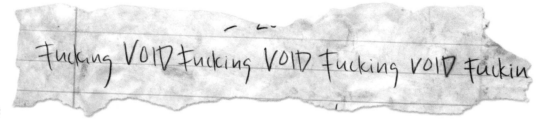
Fucking VOID Fucking VOID Fucking VOID Fuckin

24 May 1988

Boredom. Sad.

Hi. My heart hurts. I haven't written lately because I've been basically sleeping and contemplating a lot of things. I've come to the conclusion that this book is just me being a fool. I don't have anything to say.

Blah blah blah blah blah.

What's the point?

29 May 1988
4:03 a.m.

Tonight I saw the Revolting Cocks and guess who I met? David Ogilvie (Rave). Is he your brother or not? He was really sweet. The show was a bit pathetic. Three girls were on stage being perverted. I don't think I'd like to meet that Al (Jourgensen) person.

One of the girls refused to take her dress off (the other two had shirts on until Al took them off). He was practically tearing her clothes off and she ran offstage crying. I felt bad for her. The other two were blondes with tan lines and I guess the demented sex-deprived men in the audience had a good time. Burlesque and music for $15. What a deal. Blah. None for me, thanks.

Anyway, I talked to Rave after the show and he's really nice. He put me +1 on the guest list for Cleveland.

If I recall correctly, I did see Al apologizing to the girl whose dress he tried to tear off. I saw them at the side of the stage. She had her head down and he was trying to look at her face. He looked sincere, or maybe I dreamed it. I'm not too certain.

6:03 p.m.

Well, I've been working all day on my fucking design project and I'm not even close—oh, forget it. It's a waste. I hate it. I'm kind of depressed so I thought I'd pull out a Christian Death album and play it over and over and over and over and over and over and over and over. Blah. Closer. I'm going to take a nap.

31 May 1988
Revco in Cleveland

I think everyone hates me. I'm completely embarrassed and depressed about last night. For the millionth time, I made a complete fool out of myself. I went to Cleveland to see the Revolting Cocks, and well, I got really drunk and well, the place kicked me out! Can you believe innocent me got kicked out?! I've never been drunk at a show.

Anyway, I staggered around being quite stupid. Jenny looked for Rave so that maybe I could get in. I came around the corner and I saw Jenny standing with Rave and he took me upstairs. We went over to the entrance and he tried to get me in but the people kept saying, "Don't let her in, we kicked her out twice," and Rave asked if I had my ID but it didn't matter because I'm only 18. People were yelling for him because the show was about to start so he said, "I'm really sorry, I tried." Then I went outside, got sick, and cried.

Jen told me—well, she yelled at me—saying that writing to you doesn't accomplish anything, that you don't like me, that you're not going to write me back, and that if I didn't write to you, you would forget that I exist.

I walked down the darkest alley. I felt like I was going to die. I was so scared. I kept getting sick. Jen and Tracy found me and took me to get coffee. Then we sat on the sidewalk and Jen wanted to leave but I didn't want to. The show ended and I wasn't as drunk as before, so I found some guy and asked him to find Rave. I looked dead. My makeup was smeared all over the place. I probably smelled like vomit. My slip was over my skirt. Anyway, the chubby guy in the band (Luc Van Acker) came out and said, "Are you waiting for a kiss from me?" and I said "No, I'm waiting for Rave," and he said ,"You're waiting for a kiss from Rave?" and I said, "No, I have to talk to him," and he just stood there and I said, "Your name is Luc, isn't it?" and he said, "How did you know?" and I said, "I can tell by your accent," and then I said, "I saw you in Detroit. I liked your music but I thought those girls ruined it. They were really shallow," and he said, "I liked it. What does shallow mean?"

Then Rave came out and I don't remember the order but he said, "I didn't like when you said you were going to kill yourself. That upset me." I said, "I didn't say that," and he said that I did. I told him that I don't want to die and that I'm terrified of death. I could never kill myself. He said that death is inevitable and then he said, "My father died." He was being so sweet and I felt guilty for being an immature, emotional, drunk little brat.

I was telling him my fucking pathetic life story. I feel sorry for him because he listened to me. I told him that I'm a failure in school and he said, "What do you want to do?" and I said that I want to be a photographer and he said, "Then be one. You can do whatever you want to." He was giving me a pep talk. It was such a nice pep talk. I told him that I'm going to give my psychology teacher some Skinny Puppy lyrics on the last day of class and he said, "Why?" and I said "Because they're very interesting," and that when I first read them, I looked up all the words that I didn't know the meanings of and most of those words appeared in my psychology book more the once. He said, "They are intelligent but don't live by them," and I said "I don't," and he said, "Do you live by the Bible?" and I said, "No," and he said, "Then don't live by Skinny Puppy lyrics." I said, "I don't." I kept talking and talking and talking. He said, "You have a life of your own," and I said I know that, because I do know that, and I told you that I know that. Then Jen came over and said—well, she yelled at me. She said she was going to leave and Rave told me he didn't want me to get left behind and he told us he'd see us in three months. Then we left and everyone was mad at everyone. Mostly everyone was mad at me. Jenny, Kristy, Tracy, and Jen.

Jenny & Kristy

I got home at 6 a.m.—slept until 10 a.m. I felt like dying! I was so depressed. I felt so embarrassed and lonely this morning. I cried and went to work at 11. I took an early break and cried. I can't eat. I can't smile. I felt so sick. You know? I sense hate. I feel stupid and worthless.

I wanted to be raised differently. I wanted to have a father and sisters and brothers. I didn't want to be teased in elementary school. I wanted to be special. I wanted to cry less. I wanted to be disciplined. I wanted to be safe. I look in the mirror. I know myself. I don't like myself and I know you can't like myself. I don't want to die. I don't want you to dislike me. I don't know you well, but you matter. Kristy tried to tell me that I write to you because she says you're good-looking. That's so shallow and untrue. I'd write to you even if you looked like David Lee Roth but still had your thoughts. I like all nice people. I have no right to say anything to you. I have no right to care. I don't know myself and I'm sorry about everything. Really I am.

1 June 1988

NO MORE SADNESS EVER...

My book is finished. Thank you and remember I don't want to die. I'm afraid. I love my grandparents and I wish you'd share your experience "contacting your father" after he died with me. In your letter you said you'd tell me if I'm interested and I really am.

Sincerely,
Jolene Marie Siana

12 June 1988

Ogre,

Do you want to know what's wrong with me? Well, I'll tell you. My hands shake. I'm tired all the time.

I've been dwelling in the past. I've been crying for no special reason. Hours of sadness for no special reason. My insecurities are to the point where I can't even look into anyone's eyes because I fear they'll see right into me and know all of my thoughts, wishes, and dreams, and they will see that I'm stupid and twisted, and they will hate me. I experience my grandparents' death every night. I understand my life is not your responsibility, but I am so tired of having everything in my life hate me.

My mother bought me a birthday card. We got into an argument and she got all hyper and ripped it up. Fucking hilarious, isn't it? Just like my pathetic life! I hate me I hate me I hate me I hate me. So right now she's getting sick because she's drunk as usual. Ashes, ashes, we all fall down. Why are birthdays so important anyway? Why is feeling cared about so important? Some people take advantage of that and it hurts me. Yes, I show so much emotion. I'm tired of rejection. I smell her disgusting cigarettes. I'd like to smile and mean it one of these days. Everything means nothing.

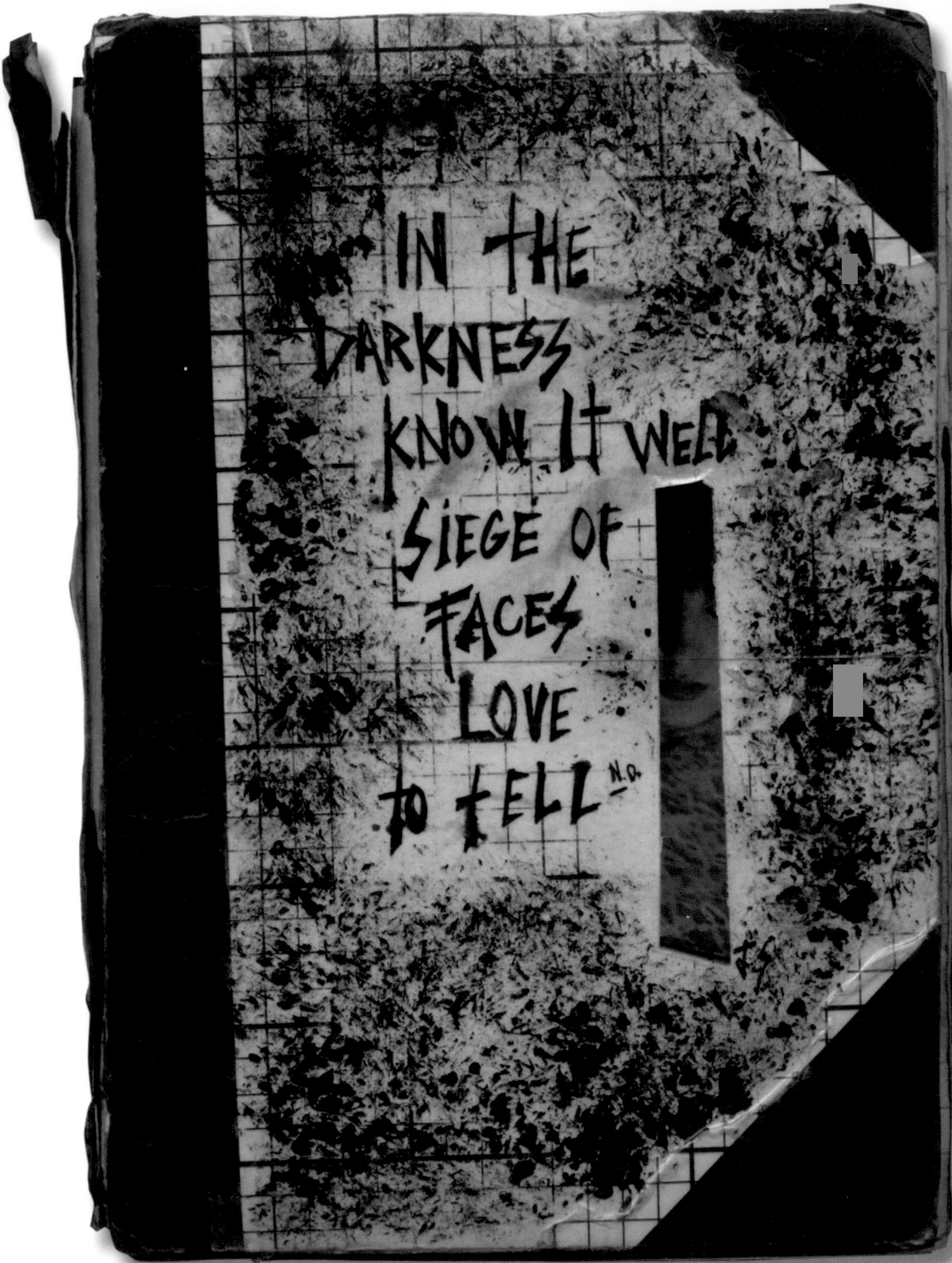

"IN THE
DARKNESS
KNOW IT WELL
SIEGE OF
FACES
LOVE
to tELL" N.O.

A plane has crashed near the Toledo airport. Too much sadness. You know how dark it is? I wish you could be here with me to see how truly dark it is.

—✦—

Let's go blow bubbles and forget about pain. I think about sleeping and never waking up. Would you like to know one of the worst feelings in the world? Just existing. You're alive. You're alive and you know it would be so easy to take a gun to your head, or to run in front of a semi.

At this moment, I'm just here. Not a care in the world. I could leave earth and not care. You know, I was doing all right mentally. The pep talk with Rave did me good. I was pretty stable, then I looked into the mirror. Not only the physical mirror but the mental mirror, and I saw myself falling. Rotting. Dying. I thought, I'll be all right, but I'm NOT. Not in any way. Oh, it's so great, this being different. No one is on my level because I <u>haven't</u> a level. I'm just kind of off to the side, away from everyone, weeping without tears. It can be done. I fall asleep and I see my bloody future. Dimmer, foggier each time. I don't like myself.

16 July 1988

Well, Tiffany came to visit. My fucked mother doesn't like Tiffany so I thought I'd clean to try to change my mother's mood. My mother didn't say anything; she's a bitch.

18 July 1988
12:15 p.m.

I'm on my break.

So at about midnight, Tiffany and I went over to Andy and Chris's and then the 4 of us went to the park to swing and told each other our worst fears, and I kept making up stories about what was going to happen to us that night, like we were going to die because the park was in a bad neighborhood. Then I was the one who started getting paranoid, of course, and the trees started looking like scary monsters, and so we went back to the apartment.

When I got up, my mother was in the kitchen saying, "I want that girl out of here." Tiffany was in the bathroom and I was defending her, and then my mother picked up this book I wanted to read because Ayse% has it and says it's great and that you've read it. *Maldoror*. She threw it at me saying, "What kind of book is this?" And we screamed and yelled at each other, then she threw water on me. I don't know if she thought I would melt or what but I was so upset.

planned with ... banks of the Maumee.

"**W**e don't just live in Toledo. We live it up!"

It's clear that Toledoans already find ... here a great place to ...

I went to work all upset. Then I was really upset on my break, so I cried and I wrote a story about how she's made me so insecure. Then after work, Tiffany and I went over to my new friend Pauline's house. It was about 9:30 p.m. and we went to my house. My mother was being the absolute worst kind of creature imaginable. Oh, I want to kill her just thinking about it. She was loudly swearing and being so fucking cruel and closed minded and I hated her. Again, those horrid thoughts entered my mind.

Tiffany walked out and I was yelling at my mom and she was saying like, "I cut you out of my will, you don't live here, I cancelled your life insurance."

#1 I don't give a fuck. I don't want her useless shit.

#2 I do live there and if she would kick me out, my aunt would give me money to live.

#3 If I die, who fucking cares because it will hurt her, not me. I'll be DEAD.

She also accused me of being a Satanist. Oh, right. I was crying so hard and my mom said she was going to lock me out. I hated her. I wanted to—I won't even put it in writing. It's awful, really. Then I got a screwdriver and I was going to detach the chain lock so I could get in, but she grabbed it from me. I went to the phone and started to call my Aunt Karen, but then my mom said, "Who are you calling now?" and my mind went blank and I couldn't make the call. Then I got another screwdriver and undid the chain lock and Tiffany kept ringing the buzzer and I was so upset. I haven't been that furious in a LONG time. So we went to get razor blades. Tiffany slashed her legs up really bad. I mean it was bad, not with razor blades—with glass. I didn't cut myself anywhere. I hurt enough. Besides, I told you NO MORE BLOOD EVER!

10:41 a.m.

Well, after 11 hours of sleep, I'm all right mentally but I'm shaking. I owe $100 for car insurance. My mother still thinks I'm evil. Oh yes, I'm so scary. I have to pause my little story so that I can say that I'm anxious to see what it's going to be like when I see you. Don't laugh at me, OK? I really don't want to hurt. When I see you, I'm going to pose as a happy kid and I hope you won't be in a bad mood. Maybe Tiffany and I will give you this new book and the flowers, then we'll get lost.

I just called my mother schizophrenic and she called me a twerp. Cute, huh? Do you like crying and the feeling in your stomach when you're crying? It's 4:24 p.m. and I thought I felt like writing but I don't.

~

18 July 1988

At Kinko's this guy that I met the other night came up to me and said, "You were at Andy's the other night, weren't you?" I said, "Yes," because I was at Andy's 3 nights last week and I didn't remember which night he was there. He said, "Are you the 17-year-old or the 19-year-old?" Then he shook my hand and started getting close to me and he tried touching my face and I turned away and he said, "What's wrong?" and I said, "Nothing," and he said, "I'm not trying to hurt you, I just think you're sweet," and he proceeded to touch my face and I backed away and he said, "Don't you trust me?" and I said, "I don't even know you," and he said, "I met you the other night," and I said, "That doesn't mean I want you touching me." And he got mad and walked away. He was an asshole.

He started talking to Jenny and she interrupted him because she was printing her fanzine and it was her turn and he got all hyper and when she asked him to continue, he refused because she interrupted him. I'm sure. We didn't go there to talk to that loser. I was copying a photo of Skinny Puppy for the story on your band in the fanzine and he said, "You're copying shit like that and you're afraid of me?" and I said, "What's your point?" and he looked at me blankly.

~

I'm working hard
I don't know why
I'm like a working class dog
And I just get by
—Rick Springfield

~

I'm in a good mood today—perhaps it's because my mother left for her vacation. She'll only be gone for 3 days, but that's 3 days of peace! Last night she was complaining about my room saying, "Is black pretty, are skulls pretty, are pictures of people with blood all over their faces pretty?" I told her that death is the only sure thing in life. Like, you can say that you're going to work tomorrow but you never know. You could die or get in a car accident and not work. You can say that you're going to do a lot of things but something could happen. When you say that you're going to die—you're going to! I was trying to tell her that all of those things that make her sick make me think, and she said that there is such thing as thinking too much and I told her that I disagree.

Did I tell you that this girl told me that I remind her of a porcelain baby doll? Isn't that funny? Someone else told me that too. La la la la la. I'm annoying aren't I?

I think you should put a warning label on *Cleanse Fold and Manipulate* telling people not to listen to "Anger" when wearing headphones, because it may cause disturbance and make you hear things you don't really want to hear. It's really intense. What's going on in the background? My eyes itch. Happiness. How long will it last? I'm going to Toronto next week, but I can't make plans because Psychee's phone is shut off (I just broke a fingernail) so I really don't know what's going on. After I get back from Toronto, I'm going to get another job and I'll work one full-time and one part-time job.

~~

19 July 1988

Lindy and I went to her house and her mother wanted a newspaper, so she let Lindy (who only has a temporary license) drive. We went to the local carryout and I thought I recognized this guy who was wearing high black boots, faded black jeans, no shirt, and had long, puffy brown hair. Kind of metal, you know? But I wasn't sure. Then he said, "Remember me?" Lindy and I had him in art class. I remembered and we were at the checkout counter and he was walking out but he kept talking and I didn't know what to say so I'm like, "So, did you graduate?" and he said, "No—you?" and I said, "Yes, 2 years ago, wait, no, 1 year ago," and he said, "Almost 2 years," then he walked out and Lindy and I were done so we walked out and that guy started walking towards me and he wouldn't let me by and he trapped me against the wall and my hair was hanging over my shoulders and he was touching it and saying, "I love your hair," and I was like, "Thanks," and these girls who were with him were telling him to hurry up, so he freed me and said, "You know, I still have that shirt that you wrote your name on," and I said, "Oh, well, keep it forever," and those pseudo-blondes were making fun of me because I was wearing all black and I looked like a total scumbag. Do metal guys like that?

I remember, I probably wrote Skinny Puppy lyrics on his shirt. That's funny that he still has it, because I didn't even write it with permanent ink. I must be special to someone. Anyway, we drove around, visited Lindy's sister and her new puppy, and then we went back to Lindy's and she asked, "Am I close enough?" as she drove over the curb onto the grass. Now I'm home. I'm on the porch drinking grapefruit juice mixed with Sprite and it's good. I'm just kind of here.

Psychee & Ayse'lo... THE PENPALS in Toronto:
Ayse'lo, ME, Nicole, Jane & standing & Corinna, Psychee & Mich.

I stumble and fall over your gaze and your call
—Clan of Xymox

WHAT ARE YOU GOING TO DO?

Are you going to happen to your world? What's the point of giving up? Leaving won't change anything. What's the point of doing drugs? Leaving won't change anything. What's the point of existing? What's the point of writing? Why bother? We're all going to get old and soft anyway.

I believe in God and I pray each night for unfortunate people. Female, 19 years of age, of average intelligence. What is wrong with me? Question. I matter. I have feelings. I DO care about people and I hate seeing people suffer.

I wish I could gather all of the lonely people (children, adolescents, middle-aged adults, and senior citizens) and form a community of warmness, generosity, and happiness. Am I insane?

20 July 1988

Hi. It's 11. Working with dumb blonde Kayleigh is completely INTOLERABLE! I haven't yet had the chance to tell you about this truly sad, absentminded human. You would not believe her stupidity! She gets annoyed when I make statements. I don't care. She just lives. She's completely oblivious to anything and everything that doesn't pertain to her life.

Today she said, "I've never met anyone like you, I'm serious," and I know she meant to put me down, but I said, "I don't know how you wanted me to take that, but I'm taking it as a compliment."

She says I think too much, because I was talking about death being the only sure thing in life and she didn't like that. I was getting really sick of her STUPIDITY. So I said, "Don't you ever think? Are you never going to think? Will you always be this void with no brain?" and she said, "I have a brain," and I said, "Then try using it sometime." You really wouldn't believe it. I <u>am</u> going somewhere in life. I'm going to be somebody, unlike her and her druggie attitude. I think she's going to be a housewife. She asked me what kind of guys I like and I said, "Guys with depth," and she said, "You and your words, I don't even understand you," and I said, "You don't know what depth means?" and she said, "No," and I said, "You know, when someone is deep, when someone likes to think," and she looked at me blankly and I said, "Do you like to think?" and she kind of nodded! Stupid!

- 65 -

COMBUST

6:19 am.
I have just decided
that the most exciting way
to commit suicide would
be to go up in space —
in a shuttle or something
+ jump out + see
the world + evaporate.
or something

Along the seawall but stuck in the grid: *Battery May 5, 1986*

Using black glop, Donald Sultan produces gloomy elegance

I never thought people like that would have to exist in my life! When I yelled at her today she told me not to worry about her and I said, "I'm worried about you and all the other Kayleighs in this world." She didn't catch on. Oh well, life is hell.

⟞⟝

Question my insanity.

22 July 1988

I live by an "old folks home" and I always see this man walking his wheelchair. He looks so sweet. I saw him this morning at about 8:30 sitting in his wheelchair watching cars go by. I'm in a pleasant mood and I really don't feel like talking about depressing things, but anyway, I want to talk to him. Poor old people. They've lived for so long and they have all of these memories without anyone to share them with. I just feel so sorry for them. I'm afraid of growing old. I'm afraid of dying.

Last night, I dreamt about my paranoia of death. I can't get away from it. Maybe in 20 years you will read this and I will be dead. Perhaps in 2 years. Could be one day after you read this, before you get to this page and even before I finish this book. I'm just taking one day at a time. They tell you to do that in Alcoholics Anonymous. They should organize a Scared of Dying Anonymous.

⟞⟝

23 July 1988

I talked to God last night. I asked him why people had to hurt so much and why old people are lonely and why people do drugs and why they steal and kill and hurt people's feelings and why people die and why they hurt and hurt. Then I went to sleep.

I woke up this morning. This mourning. Not looking forward to this day. I had to look all over the fucking house to find something clean to wear. I put my shirt on the ironing board and I turned the iron on. When I returned I found an opened letter from Tiffany lying on my shirt. I looked at my mother and asked if she read it. She said YES and I got really angry and told her she has no right. Of course she misinterpreted it. Although Tiffany did mention cutting her legs with glass. Tiffany is self-destructive, but that doesn't make her a bad person. She is, in fact, one of the sweetest people I know. Even after my mother created that big scene when Tiffany visited, she did not even once call my mother a bitch or say anything negative at all. My mother is evil.

Well, during my brief insanity, I took a new jar of peanuts that was nearby and poured the majority on the floor. My mother demanded me to pick them up. I did not. I went into my room and got the paper that I had written for my mother. It's my whole life. Why I'm insecure and why it's her fault.

26 July 1988

Not like you care or anything but my world is falling apart. Falling. Falling. Falling. Falling. Anyway, fuck, you know. I don't care about anything. I don't care about this notebook. I don't care about this life. You know what? I don't even care if you hate me! See, see how I can change? I haven't changed though. It's always been here. I am uncaring. Not sincere enough—I have been accused of being a fucking Satanist. Oh yes. I'm sooo evil. I'm tired.

30 July 1988

I'm getting along with Kayleigh in snack bar hell (work), but she's still not too bright. There was a fly in the onion

blah. July 26th view from my porch on a Foggy morning. mourning

container overnight and I was saying that I hoped that there were no maggots, and she said, "It's a FLY!" and I said, "Maggots become flies!" and she was like, "Really?"

2 August 1988

Now my mom is listening to Roger Whittaker whistle "Lullaby and Good Night" and she's crying and I wish my life would fucking be normal. I'm not like her, understand?

〜〜

I'm so sick of me, I'm so sick of trying.
I'm so sick of hurting
I'm tired of crying.
—Jolene

〜〜

3 August 1988

The hills are alive. Magic words. I should be happy. This girl that I work with here asked me if I write from the time I wake up until I go to bed. I said, "No," but I practically do. Killer. This photographer from California is here today. He said "Killer." Just say no.

〜〜

Richard hung himself.
Richard hung himself.
It happened just the other day.
Death the final high.
Throw it all away.
Throw it all away.
— D.I. (from *Suburbia*)

17 August 1988

Wow. Look where I spent my day: Lansing, Michigan, checking out a school. More to come! I'm going to Pittsburgh and Philadelphia this week, Detroit next week and possibly Dayton soon too. Anyway, it was loads of fun here. So I exaggerate.

I was conceived in Lansing! Mistake?

19 August 1988

I'm in Flushing, Michigan, now. I'm staying with my aunt and uncle. At about 10:30, Brian (my cousin) and I went bike riding. We went by 2 ex-girlfriends of his. He told me about his "love life." Kind of strange, though, because he's 11 years old, and he's talking about his former girlfriend's bedroom.

We went swinging. I heard drums and Brian told me that there's a pit nearby where Satanic rituals go on. Whatever. Blah. I'm tired. I suppose I'll go before I die.

Remember my cousin Mark that loves me so much? Well, he just stated that he hates me because I wouldn't get off the couch so he could do flips. Anyway, I spent like 1½ hours picking blueberries in the sun. Last night Theresa and Julie came over. I'm upset because the Flint newspapers don't have the cartoon The Far Side.

8:34 p.m.

Well, I went over to a neighbor's house with my aunt. We talked about wills, funerals, cremation, and cemetery lots. It was interesting. Then I played with her 8-month-old baby girl, then I came home and the dogs looked bored, so I tried playing catch but they got too wild. Don't you miss the days when you still believed in Santa Claus?

Hello, it's 12:53 a.m. Well, today I went to the dentist. Last time I was there I was a freshman in high school. I was 14 years old. I'm 19 now. It's been 5 years. When I went at that age I had one cavity. I never got it filled so this morning I was a bit worried. I figured since I chew a lot of gum and drink a lot of pop (even diet causes decay) that I'd have a lot. But guess what? I only have one. He said my teeth are in good shape. Goody.

Fuck this! I am so fucking sick of this! We're packing things into the van. My aunt is taking me to see more schools, and bringing the whole family with us. We're picking my mother up in Toledo. My aunt is rushing. All of my things are packed. Ready to go. My aunt asks Brian and Mark to get their shoes. "No, we're watching *Dennis the Menace*."

Uncle enters.
Uncle Bob: Jolene, are you going to eat?
Jolene: No, I'm not hungry.
Uncle Bob: You better eat.
Jolene: I can live on one meal a day. I'm not hungry!
Uncle Bob: Yeah, but then you get sick.
Jolene: All right. I'll make a salad.
Uncle Bob: Brian, get your shoes for your mom!
Brian: No!!!
Argue. Argue. Argue.
Aunt Karen: Jolene, I'll take care of it.
Brian: No, mom, we're watching *Dennis the Menace*!

Uncle enters again. At this point I'm eating my salad, so I can finish and get the hell out of there. My uncle hits Brian and yells and screams the way my mother did when I was his age. I start feeling bad. Not hungry. Can't waste, they're tight with money. Brian cries and runs upstairs. Mark turns the television on again. I'm sad. My uncle says, "Jolene, you can at least wait until we're ready to eat!" I jump out. I'm out of there. Now tell me why in the fuck would I want to wait until everybody has their bloody hamburgers in front of them so they can be pissed off and yell with their mouths full and completely nauseate me? WHY?

Do—a deer, a female deer
Re—a drop of golden sun
Me—a name I call myself
—The Sound of Music

25 August 1988
2:20 p.m.

McDonald's salad breakfast. McDonald's salad lunch. Blah. I refuse to eat a McDonald's salad for dinner. Injured plea. Pittsburgh was nice. It seemed safe. I'm drinking and spilling water all over this page. I apologize.

3:35 p.m.

Want to hear something funny? My mother told me that my relatives in New Jersey think I'm "punk." Ugh, my cousins are really getting on my nerves. I didn't want them to come in the first place! I love them, but I love them more when I haven't seen them in a while! Brats. Brats. Brats. Brats. Brats. Brats. Slow hate building. We passed a bad accident site.

Mark is unbearable. He's whining and crying and getting his own way the whole way and he's going to turn out like Brian. She's defending him because he's 7 years old. Fuck that. I never saw anything stating that all 7-year-olds should be spoiled little pigs. Fuck you Mark. I hate this. This trip is supposed to be for me. Fucking brat. Oh, she's sacrificed so much so that we could make this trip. I HATE I HATE. Little spoiled fucking brats grow up to be big spoiled fucking brats. I don't think I ever want to have children. I've been thinking that ever since I moved in with my aunt.

7:00 p.m.
Philadelphia, PA

On a balcony at a restaurant hearing a protester scream his lungs out over *The Last Temptation of Christ*.

Brian & Mark

1:00 a.m.

Well, I had fun. We met my cousins from New Jersey at this restaurant. My cousins talk funny. They say car like you say "core," and they talk fast. Renee says "schiz out" or "schized out" like "freak out" or "weird out."

26 August 1988
5:54 p.m.

Hi Ogre,

We're going to a place called Butler, Pennsylvania. Nice place. Golf course, water slide. Ha ha. Brats. Loud. Brian is annoying. He is always saying, "Badness," it's more like "Stupidity!" It's muggy out. Blah, yuck!

Hello, it's later. My cousins went swimming and played video games and drank iced tea. I got my name on the screen twice playing Centipede. Proud of me?

Anyway, I'm in a pizza place with everyone. While I was lounging on the bed my mother said, "You never used to be so white. Do you put white makeup on your arms?" and I said, "No," and my aunt said that it's my diet. Because meat can make you yellowish. I think it's neat that since I mainly eat salad my skin tone is lighter.

Once, when I was about 15, I made up this crazy diet and all I ate was carrots and all I drank was iced tea. My skin turned orange! My mother called a doctor and he said that my body built up an addiction so I had to slowly withdraw from them. Funny, huh?

It's so early and I don't like it here. I cut my thumb. Razor blades. Kiss. Kiss. Well, here I am sitting alone in a Best Western bathroom so that I can write to you. Fun? Not really. My mother said that if it gets to be too much in Flushing, I can move back home. I don't know. What I do know is that I'm not tired and I feel ridiculous writing to you in the bathroom. Everyone thinks I'm crazy. I write too much. My aunt says that I spend 80 percent of my time writing. Oh well, life is hell.

Good Night.
Jolene

28 August 1988

We're back. I can tell that my aunt and cousins are sick of me, but do I care? Argue, argue, argue. Happy-go-lucky pre-pubescent brat Brian is listening to Bon Jovi on full blast and I think I'm going to vomit.

BRAT. Now he's playing air guitar. Oh Brian, you're so cool. I'm so glad they'll be starting school on Tuesday. Mark just asked if he could look at this book and I said no and he stuck his tongue out at me. Arghhhhh. Brian is singing to the Fat Boys. He's doing the actions too. Thinks he's cool. Not quite.

I am so close to moving back to Toledo. I'm really beginning to hate it here! I may possibly be getting a job so things are fucked. Tiffany sent me a poster of Johnny Depp.

᭣᭣ ᭣᭣

I'm ugly I'm ugly I'm ugly I'm ugly I'm ugly I'm ugly I'm ugly I'm ugly

᭣᭣ ᭣᭣

I'm tired of you and the things you do and all the things you say
No more babysitting for neurotic girls today
—Ministry

30 August 1988
9:12 p.m.

I AM HAPPY! Why, you ask? Well, I went to Detroit to see Annie. I got my hair dye and a pair of imitation patent leather boots. I also called Nettwerk and I didn't talk to George but I talked to Dan and he gave me the wonderful news that you're playing Detroit—at St. Andrews even! I'm really happy about that. All right. Now I am at the Hot Rock Café. Having lots of fun. Actually, I just got here.

Of course I am not dancing. Just here being my introverted little self. I'm wearing my new boots. They're quite squeaky! People are giving me strange looks. I'm bored. Kind of happy, but bored. I wish I weren't so—wasn't so insecure. I'd really like to dance.

I like this song. Is the world really passing me by? They're playing Tackhead. We're thinking of pickup lines. Interruption. Ooh, eye contact. This must be New Order night. Theresa is teaching me how to be confident.

Theresa is dancing and I am entertaining myself. I like my squeaky boots. I saw a rainbow today. I'm excited I'm going to see you. Metal guys, pass me by please! I must look like a complete freak but do I care? No.

31 August 1988

Gee, I'm such a happy person today! So, how is your life anyway? I took a 2 hour nap. NERVES. Happy. Sad. What's a girl to do? Cry, laugh, write, sigh, grin, smile, die? My cousins are being all right. They're in school now, so I have a break. I'm just too happy.

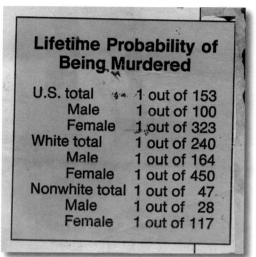

Lifetime Probability of Being Murdered

U.S. total	1 out of 153
Male	1 out of 100
Female	1 out of 323
White total	1 out of 240
Male	1 out of 164
Female	1 out of 450
Nonwhite total	1 out of 47
Male	1 out of 28
Female	1 out of 117

So I could be one out of 450. I hope I will not be killed. Drowsy. I need a job. If you're wondering where that blood came from (I don't like my scars anymore so I vowed to myself—no more razor jobs), anyway, I stubbed my toe on the front door and my toenail came off. Ugly! So the blood is courtesy of my little pinky toe on my left foot. It hurts. Hurts. Hurts. Hurts. Hurts.

Hello, well, I fucked up again. My demented little self backed out of the garage and in the process of doing so I managed to break a part of the paneling, so I'm waiting for Theresa in hopes that she gets here before my uncle gets here. I'm scared.

2 September 1988
8:55 p.m.

Hi, I'm sitting here recording Theresa some Bauhaus. She gave me 11 tapes to make! But I'm gladly doing it for her because I have my turntable and I'm happy! Gee, this book is truly falling apart.

My aunt is worried about me. Guess what? I might get to go to the Art Institute of Pittsburgh. I'm excited. I want to go there and I want to start in January. When you die, you're dead.

My aunt is entertaining tonight. I was down there, but of course I got slightly bored. I don't think my uncle wants me here anymore. Yesterday, well, I told you about the garage. Well, my uncle was really pissed because about 2 weeks ago I ran over part of his toolbox. I'm not a bad driver. That was half his fault because I told him I'd be right back. I left and when I came back, well, he shouldn't have left his toolbox in my path, right?

120

Oh well. I have to fix the garage. Can you see me with a hammer and nails? It's going to take me forever to tape her all of my Bauhaus but I don't mind. I can't wait. I can't wait. I can't wait. I took a nap and I had a nightmare!

➤➤

12:40 a.m.

Well, I really wanted to watch *Rosemary's Baby*, but Brian is still up so I have to watch *Fearless Vampire Killers*. I don't mind though. Do you think that a body could get so cold that it could break like glass? Spooky.

➤➤

NAUSEA

➤➤

3 September 1988

I wrote "nausea" last night when we went to the club after the absolute hick wedding reception. It was so disgusting. It was Top 40 and I was truly in HELL! I was also very tired and everyone thought I was trashed because I was just staring off.

Anyway, today my aunt said, "I get the feeling you don't want to stay here anymore." Gee, I wonder what gave her that idea? Well, she went on to say that she doesn't want me to leave. She thinks my mother will destroy me by...her destructiveness, and that is probably true, but it's hell here. I don't have a job. I have one friend, so to speak. I just want to go home. My mother called today and there is a great possibility that I will go to Pittsburgh in January for school.

Hi, guess what? I went on a shopping spree. I got 3 dresses, a cardigan sweater, and a purse. A lot! My aunt bought most of it. Oh, I also got a winter coat. You know, it's almost definite about me going to school in Pittsburgh. I'm glad. I hope Tracy goes there. It would be nice for me to know someone there, especially when it comes to having to share a room with someone. I've ALWAYS had my own room and I just can't imagine sharing with someone.

I don't know if I want to go to the club tomorrow. It's paranoia time again. I don't want to die before I see you. My vinyl boots cracked! I'm upset. I can't believe that I miss Toledo. Can you? My aunt doesn't want me to move back because she thinks my mother will bring me down. My mom called me last night. I think she misses me. Why is life so hard?

I'm going out tomorrow to fill out job applications. I am sick of filling out applications. I'm getting tired. My throat hurts and my hands are cold. I took Kelly (dog) for a walk today. It was neat taking a dog for a walk, like it was my dog! You know I always wanted a "family" and that was one reason why I moved here. But it's strange. I think my aunt spent all her money on me because I was depressed yesterday. I didn't ask her to buy me all of what she bought me, she just did. My life is screwed. I don't understand it.

I may have a job. Let's hope. If I do get the job and I don't have to work this weekend, I'm going to Toledo. I do hope I get the job. I hate being poor. I'm getting my facial tomorrow. Yay. I'm looking hideous lately. I'm tired. Good night.

4 September 1988
8:00 p.m.
Hi Ogre,

Nice day. I had an interview scheduled at 10:30, so my aunt wanted me to meet her at the mall to get some clothes. So we're in Express trying to find something. I've found enough. I can't believe my aunt spent so much money on me! Like $59 for a sweater, two $22 shirts, a $48 sweater, and if that wasn't enough, this evening she handed me a Hudson's bag with a $62 sweater and a $42 shirt! I feel so bad that she's spending so much money on me. Only rich girls deserve nice clothes.

I went to get my facial and I felt strange. It's in this designer place. Rich people talking about their trips to Ireland, Scotland, Florida, and California. Scuba diving, snorkeling, and such. Definitely not where I belong. I looked like a clown! The woman is nice but she said, "Oh, you're so pale, we must use the lightest shade of base make-up." She put so much on it was awful. She complimented my eyes. She called them "pretty green." Ugh, she put blush on me. I do not touch the stuff. It was a horrid experience. My uncle liked it. Blah. He nicknamed me "dragon lady."

Wow, I'm almost done with my third book. I'm happy. I bet you're not. I bet you're hoping I quit writing. You know, I'm going to feel so stupid when I see you because you haven't written and you probably hate my guts.

6 September 1988
11:34 p.m.
I'm going to bed. I called my mother and she was saying that not eating meat can do serious damage to your body and that her friend's doctor says she should eat meat two times a week at least. I refuse to eat the stuff. I will not eat meat again. If I die in that way I will not mind. GOOD NIGHT.

4:21 p.m.
Rhonda called today and she said that Skinny Puppy tickets for Detroit went on sale yesterday. $14! That's a lot! I'm FUCKING BORED. I watched *Chinatown* today. I was in a good mood yesterday. Why so sad today? I just wonder about myself sometimes. Wonder. Wonder. Nice language. Mine. Mine. Go out of my head. Exciting? Not very.

I called Jenny and told her that I'm coming home. She was happy. I also called my mom, she was like, "Oh, all right." I'm really paranoid! What if I die on my way "home?" Or on the way back? What if my car blows up with me inside? What if my books get destroyed?

8 September 1988

Ogre,

Hello. It is nighttime. I'm getting ready to go to bed and tomorrow I shall visit Toledo. I hope I don't die. I don't like driving long distances alone. Oh well. You know how it is. I'm going to offer to do major cleaning at my mom's house for money. I hope she lets me. I'm very low on money. I have absolutely no income. Good night.

11 September 1988
Sunday
Flushing, Michigan
7:46 p.m.

Unfortunately I'm back and this is hell, you know. I shall tell you about my adventure in Toledo.

On the way there I got off at a wrong exit. I went to Franklin Park Mall to return my boots and as soon as I got there I saw my friend Shaun (Suzanne's husband). Then we saw Andy, so we hung out for a while. Anyway, then I went to Hills and I talked to Kayleigh (airhead). Then I went to my mom's apartment and then I went out to eat with my mother. Then I went over to Lindy's house and we just taped videos. I didn't get home until 5AM. You're thrilled, I'm sure. I got up at 10 a.m. on Saturday and I cleaned my mother's house. Oh, on Friday night I got a nosebleed. I haven't had one of those in a long time.

On Saturday night, I went to dinner with my mother again. Jarrod took me to a party. It was OK. A lot of people came up and hugged me. It was strange. About

Jenny in my room

6 people asked for my address. I'm sad and confused about EVERYTHING.

Jenny showed up and she was mad because I wasn't home and she kept calling, but I did leave a note on my door. I want to go home. When Jenny took me home last night she apologized for being mean to me. She said it's because she misses me.

I want to go home! My aunt is being "moody" and she's bitching at me. No one here was glad to see me return. On Friday when I visited Hills I saw the general manager. He asked how I'm doing and I told him that I still didn't have a job and he said if I go back to give him a call! I want to go back. Perhaps after you tour. Maybe even before. Life is fucked. Everyone was so nice last night. What have I done? Why did I do it?

I'm going to see you soon. I'm scared. It's nerves.

14 September 1988

YOU CANNOT ALWAYS FROWN. YOU CANNOT ALWAYS SMILE.

Ogre,

Hello. Well, today is supposed to be the second coming of Christ. The end of the world. What? That's what they say. I spilled soup on myself this evening. Blah, yuck. It's in my hair. Brian is outside with some girls. How cute. My cousin gave me his Rick Springfield tape. The girl brought her pregnant dog over. It's cute. The kitchen stinks. I am bored. The light is flickering. I'm going to sew tonight. I have dog hair all over me. I'm wearing a sweater dress. I hope the soup will come out. I'm wearing this dress for the first time.

My aunt said that sometimes I act really confident. Good? Bad? Is it better to think that you're better than the norm or lesser than the norm? Prostitutes in Toledo are getting in trouble.

I went to the mall and filled out applications. I went to this cookie place and the lady sat me down at a computer and I did an interview. It was a strange interview. I was asked questions such as, "Are you lonely even when you're with a group of people?" The answers you could choose from were:

a) Occasionally

b) Never

Strange. As I was leaving she gave me a cookie. Like I needed it. I hope I get hired somewhere. I cleaned when I got home.

15 September 1988

ogre,

i'm not using capitals because i don't have the energy.

this is getting to be so discouraging. i have filled out so many applications. i'm so desperate. i may have to go home to toledo for a job.

i've applied at: frank's nursery (not just 1, but 2 locations), best, children's palace, toys 'r' us, kids 'r' us, musicland, etagé, big boy (and again, not just 1, but 2 locations), meier's (ditto), j.c. penney, bulk food, cpi photo finish, bavarian deli, pizza hut, burger king, mrs. fields cookies, village cleaners, family dining, denny's, some yogurt places...

BLAH.

10-9-88

My life in
Flushing Michigan
and other thrilling
stories — Jms

eternal flowers for you

18 September 1988

Brian is a pig and I'm going "home" soon. I called my mother last night. We argued, of course, because she said if I come back she doesn't want any of my friends there. I have a feeling I won't be too happy in Toledo but I need a job. I'm going to call the general manager of Hills today.

20 September 1988

Well, Ogre, it's Tuesday September 20 and Wendy's hired me. Blah. I don't think I want to work there. I think I'll just go back to Toledo to be put down constantly. Crushed self-esteem. Nothing. My aunt doesn't want me to go back. I just can't see myself working at Wendy's. BLAH. I'm sad.

23 September 1988

The babysitting experience was all right. I did tell you that I'm babysitting. now, didn't I? Well, I am. For a little girl named Julie. Anyway, I made $22.50 today. I'm also going to work at Wendy's and clean my aunt's house. I called Ayse% today. We were happy. I'm truly sorry, but I am quite happy.

I had to tell the lady that I'm babysitting for that I have to take a week off in October and she asked why and I told her. She asked what kind of band Skinny Puppy is and I didn't know what to say. Her children like me. I only watch the one little girl for the whole day, but I watch 3 others when they get out of school. Two boys and another little girl.

Tammy and Reverend Jim Bakker

All right. It's about 8 p.m. I have another job that pays $50 a week. I have to clean my aunt's house and I guess I'm going to take that job at Wendy's.

26 September 1988

Hi,

When I go to school, I probably won't get to write you all that often. The sad part of it is that I shall miss it more than you. I will see you soon, then it will be over and I will go to school and have a real life and even though you won't get a letter every time you visit Nettwerk, please keep me in your disturbed thoughts.

OK? OK? And when you're old and gray and sitting in your rocking chair reading old "fan mail," wonder if I'm alive. OK? And tell your grandchildren that there are some truly strange people in this world!

2:56 a.m.

ARGHHHH!

I cannot sleep! I'm just too nervous and too happy. See what you've done to me? Insanity. I've had the lights off since about 12 a.m. and it's 3 a.m. and I have to get up at 6 a.m. It's just my fault for being so happy. When have I ever been so excited? I can't even dream. I want to dream. I don't want to die.

What can I do? I want to sleep. I can't sleep. Well, my foot is asleep. I guess that's a start!

Good night. Sweet dreams. Any dreams. Sleep.

3:40 a.m.

Restless.

Why am I still conscious? Blah. I tried counting heartbeats per minute. I counted 68 one minute and 70 the next but I got paranoid because both times it seemed like I skipped a few beats. So here I am. Awake and not liking it. I was thinking about reading the dictionary but I decided against it. I want to sleep. 2 hours. 2 hours.

This is quite annoying. And it's very unfortunate that I'm going to be very busy today. I babysit until 3 p.m., then I have to go to the Wendy's office at 4:45 p.m. Then I have to go to the mall to look at my proofs and then to come home and do my daily chores. Do you predict a silly Jolene or a grumpy Jolene? I might as well stay up but I want to sleep.

5:20 a.m.

Here I am, still awake. I just remembered why I can't sleep. I took 2 diet pills after dinner. I'm starting to get shaky. Silly, stupid me.

9:15 a.m.

Yuck! All of the sudden I have a cold. Now I could fall asleep. I'm exhausted. I even passed the house on my way here. I am not with it!

27 September 1988

I picked up my beautiful Wendy's uniform yesterday. I start tomorrow. I'm excited. Ha! No, I'm not. I didn't make up all of the sleep I missed. You're not supposed to anyway. Threatening. You know, I don't know why I write to you.

29 September 1988
1:35 p.m.

Babysitting. Yesterday I worked at Wendy's and it was pretty much your fast food hell. It's yucky. I only worked for 2 hours and 45 minutes. Some guy told me I have pretty eyes. Anyway, I don't intend on working there for too long.

Oh, the other day I had some videotapes with me and Julie asked what tape I was going to put in. I told her that I had Love and Rockets and then I said, "Or I could play Skinny Puppy." And we sat there for a few minutes and she said, "Will you put Skinny Dog on?" So I did and I asked her if she liked it and she said, "Oh, I thought it would be a cartoon." It was cute.

My Flushing home

30 September 1988

Well, it was foggy this morning and a lot of business fuckheads were really annoying on the highway. I got here and the dog started crying and urinating for some reason. I was comforting the dog and I got dog urine on my pants.

She's lost control again. My eyes are starting to itch. Soaking wet. I'm going to Toledo next Saturday. Just for the day. I haven't heard your new album yet but I know it's out. I get to leave soon.

1 October 1988
10:56 p.m.

Well, another Saturday evening with the boys. We went to some laser show. Today I was quite sad. I don't know why, but I kept thinking of really negative things. I thought of positive, happy, warm things that made me sad. For instance, my grandparents' house. I'm OK now but the feeling was so empty. Hollow. Lonely.

I love: alone, together, laughing, music, candles, friends, shows, writing, long hair.

2 October 1988
Sunday

I went to church today. Nothing too thrilling. I was a spectator. I only went because Friday will be 2 years since my grandma died. Anyway, I just continue to live.

Stupid! I just got into an argument with my uncle about how brainless and untalented Whitney Houston is, although she has a pretty face and nice voice. My uncle went on to say that his opinion is obviously better than mine because the critics feel the same as him.

I just got yelled at because I started crying for no reason. My aunt thinks I get too depressed too often. And I don't think I do. I'm just sad today. Right now I'm just existing. I have been happier, haven't I? She wants me to keep a log of my depression. Blah. Such a happy piece of paper ruined. I apologize.

I suppose I ought to clean my "room." It's bothering my aunt. Her closet is in here, so she's always cutting through.

I love you, grandma and grandpa. Take me with you. What I really, truly need is a nice, friendly hug. Oh, I forgot to tell you that today is RESPECT LIFE SUNDAY. So they said at church. I'm sorry, God. I haven't done so well today.

My ear is infected and I will see you in 19 days.

3 October 1988

Head caves in.
Growing pains.
No time to see reality.
—Skinny Puppy

Grandparents House

Grandpa

Grandma & Me

8:55 p.m.

No one wants me around anymore. Everyone in this household is in a bad mood. What else is new? Darby bit my nose. They tried, they tried in vain. Dark blood rain.

9:32 p.m.

Well, I got into another argument with my uncle. It was about my hair. I'm getting blue streaks in a few days and I was telling him about it and my uncle was like, "You're not going to live here," blah blah. He was making fun of my way and I got mad. He was saying that I can't babysit with blue and black hair and that I definitely can't work at Wendy's and I was upset at this point and I walked out of the kitchen saying, "FUCK WENDY'S!" I had a really awful headache so I tried to take a nap. He came up later and apologized. Chris called. He has your new album. He got it free from Capitol. He lied to them. Such is life.

6 October 1988

I got your new album and 12-inch yesterday. It's nice. I really like it. I've been studying the lyrics.

> *We all need somebody to lean on.*
> —Bill Withers

7 October 1988
2:19 p.m.

Two years since my grandma died. I found out at about 4:30 p.m. or so. That was the lowest point in my life. Not now.

Last night I listened to *Vivisect VI* with the lights off. I like it a lot. Headphones in bed. Nice and warm. Close yet cold. I heard Roman vomiting.

Do you understand yourself?

11:02 p.m.

"You like all those weirdos." – Uncle Bob

9 October 1988

Fascinating to see the people whose blood you share, yet nauseating because you share their blood. I went to Toledo for my family reunion yesterday. All right.

I went over to Lindy's and we went to Jonathon's. I got my jean jacket. It's nice. The painting on the back is of Roman Polanski but it kind of looks like Andy Gibb, too. I like it though. In a while I'm going out with Theresa. I'm nervous about seeing you. I think you might hate me.

KEVIN - hi. george says I probably will not see you. Anyway - here i am on paper. October 14th 10:00 pm

I reali...
to give...
cross b...

coming m...
eyes. In som...
emptiness...
seems to be t...
& the small one)
These don't tak...
here now and...
someone who...
I don't believe in...
Not that i...
too hard. So...
because - you kn...
too much to do.
too soon - their...
ha...ne. I am...
hope youre forg...
might understand.
and other sp...

the cemetery is an
open spaces among the ruins
covered in winter with violets
and daisies. It might make
one in love with death ~
to think that one should
be buried in · so sweet a place.
P.B. Shelley

13 October 1988
Thursday
10:42 p.m.
Depression.

A few reasons why life is hell. Last night I was about to go to bed. I turned off the downstairs hall light and walked. I tripped over Kelly the dog, bumped my head and cut my finger on the front door. My finger hurts more than my head. Yesterday, Tony, the third grader I babysit, stayed home again. He was a brat. Today he went to school but he called and said he was sick, so I had to go get him! Then I went to this little used clothing store and put a velvet jacket on hold.

Friday 14 October 1988
7:26 a.m.

I am currently sitting at a gas station waiting for my aunt to come get me. My car died just as I was getting on the expressway. Life is hell and you know it. My fucking car. Sucks sucks sucks to eternity.

2:30 p.m.

This whole day has been HELL! Tony stayed home again, Allie stayed home and of course Julie and I feel sick! I have to be here until 4:30 then I have to work at Wendy's at 6. I got so pissed off at Tony and I had to call his mother.

George says I probably will not see you. Anyway, here I am on paper. October 14, 1988. I realize you are very busy but I'd like to give you another one of my crass book-long letters. I shall be seeing Skinny Puppy in a few cities though I don't expect anything.

15 October 1988

My aunt has just called me a FATALIST. What do you think? I guess perhaps I am. She labeled that on me when I was drinking tea and she said that it's best to drink it weak because you can get bladder cancer, plus I use Nutrasweet, and blah, blah, "It causes cancer in laboratory animals"— what else is new?

Anyway, I was saying that it would be my luck to get cancer, etc., and that life really isn't fair because I didn't ask to be born and I have to worry about life's pressures and death.

The you that lives inside the you that people see. I'm shaking, shaking, shaking, shaking. Really shaking. Scared—that too.

On my way to Toledo, my fucking tire shredded! High school guys changed it for me and I drove 70 miles with a tiny spare going only 45 mph!

It's Thursday now and I am sitting in a car service-type place. Fun fun. My rides to see you are completely screwed. I wanted to see you in Pittsburgh but blah, blah, blah. Such is my ever-so-wonderful life! At least I'm alive. Ha ha ha ha.

16 October 1988

It's a Sunday and not a pleasant one. At least it will soon be over. It started out with Brian and Mark refusing to get ready for church. Brian ran around complaining how stupid it is. I don't have to go.

I was upstairs, but I basically heard all that happened. My uncle was yelling at my cousins and my aunt tried to get them to get ready and my uncle supposedly hit my aunt. She left. My cousins are spoiled. I don't think he hit her. I would've heard it.

Oh, Wendy's called today. I was supposed to work. Oh well. I quit after working 2 days.

21 October 1988 (Journal entry)
Cleveland

Jenny picked me up at about 3. I was upset because I wanted to leave earlier because it was raining pretty badly. We got to Cleveland at about 5:30 P.M. or so. The bus was at Phantasy and I was really nervous. Jenny and I went over to the bus but no one was there so I saw this guy who looked familiar and I asked him if he was with Skinny Puppy. He was. His name was Al. I told him that I had something for Ogre and he said the band was at the hotel and he would give it to Ogre later, but I said that I wanted to give it to him. He told us to come back in about an hour and the band would be there. Jenny and I left because she wanted to eat, so we went to a pizza place. It was taking forever. We went back to Phantasy and Tracy was there.

I talked to this guy who worked there and I asked him if he would get Al. We waited at the side door and Jenny waited inside. I waited right by the door and I looked up and I saw someone that I thought was Rave, but then this person said "Jolene" and held his arms out and I realized that it was Ogre and he said, "Give me a hug," and gave me a gigantic hug. It was so sweet. He said, "So, how are you?" and I shrugged and said, "I moved," and he said, "Yeah, uh, Michigan." I was surprised and he said, "I may not write back but I do follow you." He was leaning down to talk to me and his eyes looked so pretty. I said, "I have something for you," and I handed him a bag with my book inside and he said, "A book. Great! I'm going to send those back to you someday," and I said, "Why?" and he said, "So you can remember."

I showed him the back and he laughed, then I showed him some of the "art" in my book. I opened it to the part where the "Happy Birthday" music was playing and

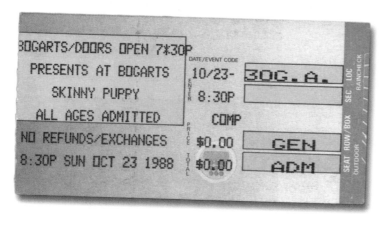

he put it up to his ear and he was singing to it. It was so cute. He asked me when my birthday is. He said that his was coming up and I told him that that's why I put that in there. He came to the part where I tore out the pages from the cult books that my mother had and I said, "My mother thinks I'm a Satanist," and he said, "My mother thinks I'm a drug addict. I don't know whether that's true or not." I had laminated the cover and he ran his fingers over it. I introduced him to Jenny and Tracy. Then he told us he'd put us on the guest list. He was in such a happy mood. I gave him Ayse%'s letter and he said, "I like her, she's cool," and I told him that I visited her and he asked how she was doing. He asked if I had the new album and I said, "Yes, it's great," and he said, "I'm glad you think so, because I was in LA and I didn't know what I was doing or where I was and I was going up and down and up and down and I was going insane." He mentioned something about a broken arm. Then he said, "I got back to Vancouver and I had to write lyrics and I couldn't write." Then he had to go do the sound check. He said that he's insane before the sound check.

This guy came back. I remembered him from last year. I said, "Are you Dan?" and he said, "Yes." I said, "I'm Jolene," and he said, " Hi Jolene, how do you do?" and shook my hand. I asked him if we could stay inside for the sound check and he said yes. Then this blonde girl came back and said hi. I assumed she was with Ogre. She came back later and asked us if we were all right. Somehow Texas came up and I asked her if she was with the opening band and she said, "No, I'm with Ogre." Anyway, then we had to leave.

We went out front and when the doors opened our names weren't on the list, so we went around back and gave the promoter our names. When we went around to the front again, they were there. I saw Al and he asked if we got in all right and he said, "Ogre wants to talk to you," and I was freaking out but I said, "Yeah, we talked to him." So, we went in front. This place was so big, so I talked my way to the front and Skinny Puppy came on. It was awesome.

After the show, we went upstairs. We didn't see anyone but then the lead singer from the opening band walked by and we asked if we could go back with him and he said, "No." Just then Dan walked by and said, "Jolene, come in," so I went in and Ogre came over to me and Dan was asking me if I wanted anything to eat or drink. I asked Ogre if I could get a picture with him, and he said sure. When I was putting my flash on, I was talking to Ogre and this guy came over to me and he said, "Do you squeal?" and I said, "What?" and he said, "Do you squeal?" And Ogre said, "Don't mind Larry. He's weird."

22 October 1988 (Journal entry)
Detroit

Next morning. Brian and I met Tiffany and Kim at Franklin Park Mall, then went to Annie's in Grosse Point. We shopped. I was anxious to get to St. Andrews even though it was early. We hung out at Greek Town for a while, then we went to St. Andrews. cEvin Key stuck his head out of the bus window asking if we had any pot. Then I saw Ogre. He came out and said that he put me +1 on the guest list. He was standing next to me and he had red roots. I asked him if it was his natural hair color and he said, "Which color?" and I said, "The red," and he said, "No," that his natural color is like a mousy brown and he got really close to my face and asked if mine is natural. He was talking about my jacket and he said I should've put "Simone" (from The Tenant) on it. He said he was going to see Pumpkinhead that night. He's been waiting for a year. Ogre had to go make a phone call, so we all went outside again. Cyan came out with a bucket and asked if I wanted to dig dirt with her for the stage show, so I did.

We were waiting in line and we were right up front. Dan looked out and said, "Where is she?" then he looked right at me and said, "Oh, there you are," and he handed me 2 backstage passes. I was so happy. At about 11:30, Skinny Puppy came on. At the end of the show someone threw a beer bottle and it hit Dwayne on the head and cut him. cEvin Key came out and announced that he'd have to go get stitches. Then Ogre came out highly pissed off and screamed at the audience. People were screaming, "One more song," and Ogre said, "Get us the fucking beer bottle guy and we'll do one more song." So, they found the guy and took care of him physically.

Tiffany and I didn't know what to do so we waited by the backstage doors and Dan said, "Hi Jolene." I asked him if Dwayne was all right and he said, "Yeah, it looked pretty gruesome at first, but he's going to be all right."

When we went backstage, a bunch of people were crowded in front of Ogre, so I didn't even try to talk to him. Then I tried to talk to Ogre, but my words were jumbled.

Then the news came that the dog (from the stage show) was stolen. Dan had to kick everyone out and he told me that he'd talk to me tomorrow because this news was pretty traumatic. Ogre walked by with a group of people. He was really out of it. I felt bad. Then we took off. We got to Toledo at about 5 a.m. and we went to Denny's. We were going crazy trying to figure out how to get to Cincinnati. Kim had to work. After hot chocolate we drove to Lima. It took forever.

23 October 1988 (Journal entry)
Cincinnati

When we finally got there at about 7:30 a.m. I couldn't sleep, so I got dressed and we decided that we had to take a bus. I got my pictures developed and we took a 1:30 Greyhound. Got to Cincinnati and took a taxi to Bogart's. It took forever to find someone to talk to. I saw Skully with the (fake) dog and I said, "Oh, you found him," and he was petting it and he said, "It's Chud." I petted Chud and asked for Dan but he wasn't around. Finally Dan came out back. I told him how Tiffany and I took a Greyhound and he said he'd put us on the guest list and that we could still use our backstage passes. We went to the front of the venue and got our complimentary tickets. I was first on the list.

Skinny Puppy were really good that night. After the show I saw these people from Detroit and they offered to drive me and Tiffany home because it was on their way. We went downstairs to go backstage and waited. Then these people said that the police were there and I was really confused and they told us to leave so we went out front and got in Oliver and Shauna's car and we saw the police put cEvin Key and Ogre and Dan in the cop car! I freaked. Someone at the club had called the police saying that Skinny Puppy were mutilating a dog on stage! I was so upset because animal liberation is something that Ogre obviously feels strongly about. Oliver followed the police and I was crying.

When we got to the station, I didn't want to get out of the car. But we did and waited and waited. Some guy kept checking out the charges and bail and he told us what was going on.

We went back and he explained that the charges were "drunk and disorderly" and said that Dan's bail was $65 and that Ogre and cEvin Key's bail was $1,500 each, so we figured we'd get Dan out because he's the manager. I had to give the man my driver's license and I had to sign papers. Everyone contributed.

So we waited. Some cops were escorting Dan out and he looked at me and smiled. He said, "Jolene, what are you doing spending all of your money on me?"

The officer was asking Dan if he could put me up for the night so I could get my refund the next morning in court and Dan said yes. He was talking nicely to the officers. The officer told me that I'd have to come back the next morning at 8 and Dan said that would work out because they had to be back at 9 to go to court. We had to wait a bit and

2917.11(B)   DISORDERLY CONDUCT
(WHILE INTOXICATED)

CASE NO. 88CRB 29110

COMPLAINT
HAMILTON COUNTY MUNICIPAL COURT

STATE OF OHIO vs. .... KEVIN OGLIVIE

.... PO .... ly cautioned and sworn, deposes and says that .... KEVIN .... ut 10-23-88 .... in Hamilton

County, and State of Ohio, while .... PRESENCE OF TWO OR MORE PERSONS ENGAGED .... SENSIBILITIES, WHICH CONDUCT KEVIN IN CONDUCT LIKELY TO CAUSE .... KNOWN WAS LIKELY TO HAVE SAME OGLIVIE IF HE HAD NOT .... PHYSICAL HARM TO ANOTHER contrary to and in EFFECT, CREATE A CONDITIO .... MEANOR OF THE 4TH DEGREE

violation of Section 2917.11(B) of th ....

The co ....

Sworn ....

Filed ....

By ....

INSER ....
²⁰"(in a public place) (in the presence of two or
ance) (cause alarm) to persons of ordinary .... presented a risk of physical harm ....
have known was likely to have some effect" or .... orderly conduct after reasonable warning or
(another) (property of another)"
²⁰"minor misdemeanor" or "misdemeanor of the ....
request to desist

Form S-120 BRO   CONTROL NO. ....   REPORT NO. ....

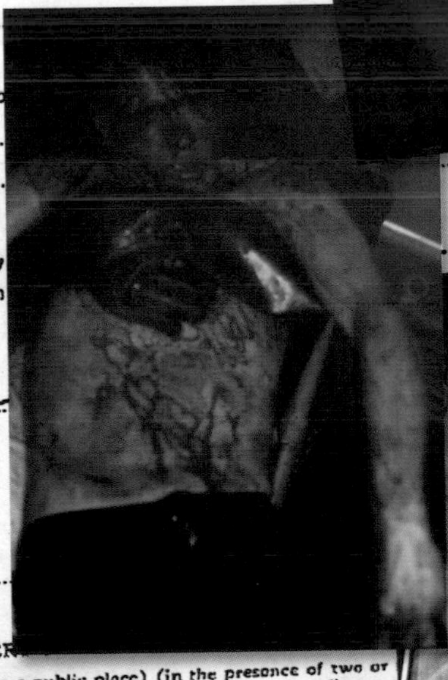

Virisect VI Tour 1988

then Ogre and cEvin came out and Ogre was talking to some fans who were waiting. He came over by me but he didn't say anything. He just looked at me. Dan, Ogre, and cEvin got in a cab and Tiffany and I rode with the truck driver who was hauling all the band's gear. Oliver and Shauna had to follow but they got stopped by the police, so we had to wait. We finally got to the hotel and I wasn't sure about what was going on, so they explained to us that we could either stay in the hotel room or in the bus. I was confused about what I was supposed to do so I asked where Dan was and went to his room and Dwayne was in there and they had the porno channel on and I was asking him what was going on and he said that we would leave at about 8:30. I told Dwayne that my friend had something for him so he followed and he said that he lost a few things and he left them in Pete's room (where everyone was), so we hung out there for a while. I was looking at an atlas saying that I live in Flushing and Dwayne said, "Flushing?" He kept looking at me. At one point I went into the bathroom and when I came out Dwayne said, "She has Polanski on her jacket."

Later Dwayne asked if Tiffany and I were going to go down to the bus and we said in a few minutes. When we went down there, I knocked on the door and the guy Skully opened it and I stepped in and we just stood there and then he said, "If you're going to come in, come in." So they told us to sit down. I sat next to Greg and Dwayne while Tiffany sat next to Al. We didn't say a whole lot. We just listened. It was Skully, Al, Gary, Dwayne, the soundman, and 2 guys from the band Lesson 7. Dwayne put Public Enemy on and they acted like rappers. They were talking about Spinal Tap. They had a video camera and they were taping everything exciting.

They offered us something to drink. Tiffany and I shared a warm RC Cola. We were falling asleep. Finally we just went upstairs and slept on the floor. Pete was really nice. He offered the end of the bed to us. It was around 4 a.m. when I finally got to sleep. I woke up when someone pounded on the door. I looked out and I didn't see anyone so I went into the bathroom, and then I looked out again and I saw Ogre. I went outside

and Dan said, "Come on, Jolene." cEvin, Ogre, and Dan were in the back, so I got in the front and I felt so stupid because everyone was really tense.

Ogre said he was having a hard time breathing. cEvin was wondering if they were going to think of something to say in court. The sun was really bright.

Ogre was mad because he didn't get a wake-up call. He was saying that someone came into his room and pushed him out of bed. cEvin said he was up since 7. Then they disagreed about something. I felt really stupid. When we got there, I just walked into the building. When we got inside, Dan told me where to go, so I took care of the bail void. I got a check. They had to go into courtroom A. I wanted to see all of their names on the wall, but I could only see "Kevin Crompton" without looking obvious. So I waited and waited and waited.

Ogre came out. I sat down and Ogre was holding a drink and he said, "Hey, do you want this?" and I said, "What is it?" and he said, "Sprite." I said, "Sure." Then I started writing to Annie. Dan came up from behind me and I shoved the letter in my purse and I started shaking. Ogre said, "Thank you, Jolene," and I said, "For what?" and cEvin Key said, "What is it that you did? Bail?" and I said, "Yes." He said, "Thank you." And I think Ogre said thank you again. We started walking and Ogre asked me if I was OK. I said, "Yes," and I said, "Are you OK?" and he said he was because he got to say what he wanted to say. He sat down and I went over and asked him if he wanted to see some pictures and he said, "Sure." I showed him the photos from the Detroit show.

The cab back was a station wagon. cEvin got in the front seat. I got to sit in between Dan and Ogre.

He was talking about court and the cEvin asked me if I was from the area because they were going to be on the news. Ogre asked me if I was going to Columbus and I told him that I hoped to. He said he'd see me there and he'd put me on the guest list. When we got to the hotel Ogre grabbed my hand and kissed my right cheek and said, "Thank you, Jolene."

I went upstairs to Pete's room. I went in and they were asking what happened. Dwayne and cEvin hugged and it was so cute. They stayed upstairs with us for quite a while. When we were leaving I waved goodbye to Dan. Then we left and went to the bank to get the check cashed. I wish I could have photocopied it.

I took a picture of Cincinnati. It was sad going back. When I got home, I went to the mall to get my pictures developed. I almost fell asleep. Then I went home and stayed depressed and went to sleep.

26 October 1988 (Journal entry)

Shauna and Oliver picked me up at about 1:30. I was really excited. We got to the Newport at about 4:30 or something. Oliver parked in an illegal spot and Dan yelled "Oliver!" Oliver looked surprised. Then he said, "Tell Shauna to come too." I got out and I was really confused. Shauna wondered how he knew her name. I was wondering *why he didn't say anything to me, but when we got inside he said, "Hi, Jolene." He was practically running and we went upstairs into an office. He said, "I need you two to make a phone call for me." And he was dialing a number and Oliver said, "What's this about?" and Dan said, "May I speak to Mrs. Hunt?" and Oliver said, "Oh," like he was mad and Dan looked at Shauna and started screaming, "You guys got me into so much fucking trouble." He was going crazy. I was in complete shock and I said "Dan, I swear I had nothing to do with this," and he said, "I know Jolene, I know." Dan left the room and Shauna told me to go talk to him, but I said, "No, he's too mad." I walked out while Dan was coming back in. I told him again that I had no idea what was going on and he said, "Those two are 16 and 17 years old. They used my name and my band's name. They're not even supposed to cross the state line." I was freaking out. He said that he was in trouble with the cops because they told their parents that they were invited to go on tour with Skinny Puppy. Shauna came out and was trying to talk to me, but I told her I was too freaked out.*

Dan invited me to dinner with the band. At Street Scene, they were joking because everything on the menu had cheese on it. Ogre was playing with his food and he threw it at Dan and he fell out of his chair. It was funny. Al was saying that the last time they ate there, they had a food fight and had to pay the place $200 just to get out. I heard Dwayne say, "Jolene," so I turned around and he said, "Would you like some of my pizza because I'm sure I won't be able to eat it all, maybe that piece but nothing more. " It was so sweet. I just said, "No, thank you." Then he put down a napkin in front of me and said, "Jolene, this is fuel, you need it to live. Look, there's cheese and pineapple..." He was pointing at all of the ingredients. He looked very cute. I told him that I already ate today and he said sarcastically, "Oh, you already ate today!" He seemed kind of offended that I wouldn't take his pizza. I'm really weird about eating in front of people. Plus, I did eat that day. I had a yogurt.

People started leaving. The only people left were Ogre, Rick, some other guy, and me. We went back to the Newport.

Cyan came down and asked me if I wanted to go dig dirt with her, so I did. As we were walking out, Ogre said, "No rocks." He said it quite a few times actually. When we were outside we were talking about our fucked up home lives. I told her how my mother puts me down all the time and she said, "Look, you're beautiful," and I said, "No, I'm not." Then she told me that you have to love yourself before you can love anyone else. Blah, blah, I know. I told her that I'm 19 and she couldn't believe it. She asked me if I had a "crush" on Ogre and I said, "No," and she said, "Are you lying?" and I said, "No, it's not like that at all." I mentioned something about admiring the way he writes (his lyrics). Cyan was really caring and she even hugged me. Tiffany and I hung out with her during the show. Once we were walking by Skully and he was holding a bottle of fake blood and Cyan said, "Oh, I want some blood," and I said, "Is it edible?" and he said, "It's totally edible," so I had a little taste. Skully is so cute.

After the show Tiffany and I were trying to figure out if we were going to Pittsburgh or not. Kelvin and Boomer were going back to Toledo, so we had to decide. Also, Shauna and Oliver were getting kicked out. We decided that it probably wasn't going to happen. Ogre came downstairs and said goodbye to me. Then I said bye to Dan and I went over to Tiffany and Dwayne who were on the stage. When we were talking to Dwayne, he was saying, "I'm just a big void." He's really quite sweet. We hung out for a while, but they really wanted Shauna and Oliver to leave so we hugged everyone goodbye. We drove a bit, then we stopped to get a hot chocolate. Oliver whipped out a $100 bill and I wondered where he got it. I asked him if he sells drugs and he said that they sell coke but they only traffic it, they don't do it. I asked what coke was like and he said that it makes you feel really confident and it makes you want to open up. They said that it takes effect in 10 seconds and it's not like alcohol. You remember everything.

6 November 1988
Toronto, Ontario, Canada (Journal entry)

Skinny Puppy Kids Toronto Concert Hall

On November 4th I was taking a train to Toronto. When I got there, I was greeted by Ayse%, Psychee, and some guy with a mohawk. We were all happy. We met Jane from Brantford, Nicole from Winnipeg, Mich from Chicago, and Corinna from Brantford. There were 7 of us. We had such a fun day.

On Sunday, we got downtown at about 12. We separated. Ayse%, Psychee, and I went to the Concert Hall/Masonic Temple. We saw the Ryder truck, so Ayse% and I walked to the back and Pete was unloading and I saw Skully too. I waved to him and he looked happy.

A while later, Al and Pete came out front and so I went down to talk to them. I asked Al if I could use my pass and he said that I probably could. Pete said, "You know, you're famous." And I said, "What, Cincinnati?" and he said, "Yeah, it's in all the newspapers," and Al said, "Yeah, it says, 'Teenage girl bails out band...'" or something. I forget exactly. I think he was joking.

We waited for the rest of the day and almost got killed from all of the pushing and shoving at the entrance. Finally we got in and I know I looked like hell.

We went up to the stage. I was in the second row. Psychee was in the front. The show was so crowded. I felt suffocated, trapped, and claustrophobic. I hated it. I had to get out so I wandered around for a while and the show ended after Ogre talked about being arrested in the Midwest. When they were done I looked all over for Ayse% and

Psychee and the rest of the girls, but no one was around. I saw Cyan up on the balcony and I got her attention.

She came down and asked me if I wanted to go backstage with her, so we talked for a few minutes, then started to go back. I put my pass on and the guy wasn't going to let us back, but Pete said, "Those 2 girls are all right."

We went downstairs and there were very few people there. Ogre, cEvin Key, Dwayne. I just looked at Ogre who seemed kind of out of it. I felt really stupid, so I stood there for a moment and Dwayne was looking at me so I waved at him and he waved back. Chris Sheppard (a Toronto DJ) said that he liked the buttons on my jacket.

Mich was backstage with me because she had her backstage pass, but we couldn't find the others. We ran into Dan and I was in a panic about getting everyone backstage. He gave me 3 passes and I went to the door which led outside and I handed the passes to Ayse%, Psychee, and Nicole. The mean guy said, "NO MORE!" and I said, "Dan gave these to me and said they could come back," and he said, "I don't care what Dan said." Just then Dan tapped him on the shoulder and said, "Anyone with this girl is cool," and my friends were allowed back. Ha!

They came back. Psychee had fainted and had her head down on the table. Ogre and the rest of the band came out. Ayse% went over to Ogre and then he came over to us. I went over to cEvin Key and I said, "Hi, do you remember me?" and he said, "Of course I do, you bailed us out."

They began to kick people out, so Psychee and I went up to Ogre and he touched her arm and he said, "You take care," and he kissed her on her left cheek.

Ogre's Jacket

Then he touched my arm and I forget what he said but he kissed me on my right cheek. He had stubble. He gave me the killer sign and I gave it back to him.

10 December 1988 (Journal Entry)

Annie and I were nervous all day wondering Rave and Ogre would be at the Ministry show. We got to St. Andrews at about 6 and there were 3 girls and a guy already there.

We were sitting inside trying to keep warm. We started talking to these girls from Sarnia. We exchanged addresses. Rave walked in and I called his name. He said hi but he was in a hurry because he was late, so we had to wait outside and it was freezing. Anyway, the girls that we were talking to I had actually met on May 16, 1987 at a Skinny Puppy show. After about 5 minutes, I saw

Ogre walking down the street with some girl. I tried to hide behind Annie but Ogre caught my eye as he was walking in. I heard him say hi and I waved and he waved. I was happy!

Finally the doors opened. When Ministry came on, Ogre wasn't onstage. They did a few old songs and then Ogre came out. He was directly in front of me. People were stage diving and it was so annoying. They did a really cool version of "Smothered Hope." Some asshole stepped on my head.

Ogre & Al Jourgensen

This guy next to me was really cute and nice. Every time a stage diver would come near us, he would cover my head. Then HE got kicked in the head and I felt so bad. Wendy passed out or something and Ogre kept pointing at her to signal a roadie to help her out. People kept stage diving and I had to get out. After the show, Annie and I went over to Rave's soundboard. He asked me how I was doing and I said that I was OK. He said, "We thought we'd see you in Cleveland," and I said that I didn't go. He said it was really bad there. They played at some place I've never heard of.

Anyway, we gave him the Christmas card and the candy. He said that he loved it and he hugged me, then Annie. We asked if we could go backstage to see Ogre and he said that Al is really testy after shows, but that he'd go upstairs and ask Ogre.

Rave came back down and said, "Ogre said to send you guys up," so he took us over to the stairs and said, "These 2 are OK." When we got upstairs, not a whole bunch were there. At first I was afraid to go up to Ogre. I overheard him talking about Cincinnati. Finally he turned around and we spoke. I told him that I get to go to school and he was really happy for me. This guy wanted me to take a picture of him with Ogre so I took it. I played with Ogre's necklaces. He put his arm around me and he rubbed my arm. He just kept rubbing my arm and I felt so good. He was in a really good mood.

I wanted to leave. I don't know why. I think I always want to leave before something that I don't want to happen happens. So I talked a little more, then I went over to Ogre and said goodbye. As Annie and I were walking away, he said, "Keep writing me letters," and I must have been in shock when I looked at him and maybe he felt stupid or something because he said, "If…if you need to." I smiled and said, "I need to." I was so happy.

· CHUD ·

16 December 1988

Ogre,

I'm really cold right now. If you got my Christmas card then you know about the stray dog by where I babysit. Well, the poor thing is still alone and cold and starving. Today I fed it again. I feel so bad. I named him Chud and he answers to it. He's so friendly and cute. I just keep giving him water and dog food and pizza and bread. The thing is that he's so undernourished that they'll probably end up putting him to sleep. I wish I could keep him. He probably has parasites. It's so sad.

I played with him today and I took some pictures. He looked so sad and helpless as he curled up on the doormat. When I was leaving, he just looked at me and I got in my car and I started to drive away and he was following me. I'll probably never see him again. He's so cute. It's so sad because I think about my aunt's dogs who are fed and they're warm and they're loved, and that poor dog that didn't even ask to be born is freezing and starving to death.

20 December 1988
11:08 p.m.

Ogre,

I'm taking a break. I've been taping all of my albums all day while at the same time packing for Pittsburgh. In a little over a week, my life is going to change drastically. I'm going to be sharing a room with someone, getting a new job, and going to school. I'm nervous.

Tomorrow is my grandpa's birthday.

Kevin,

Hello. Once again—Here I am!

To tell you the absolute truth I wasn't planning on writing another "book," but I saw this composition book and I had this incredible urge to buy it—so I did!

Blah. Anyway, I'm nervous about school. Less than 2 weeks! I have to get a physical before I go. I have to do so much before I leave. I'm nervous. It's going to take me forever to finish this book! It's pretty thick. Oh, I don't mind if you return these books of my life someday. You don't even have to read the whole thing. Just glance and shelve. I'm sure anyone would be so completely thrilled to read what goes on in my life. That's a joke!

11:45 p.m.

Well, a plane crashed in Scotland. Pretty sad. Its final destination was Detroit. It's just really sad, especially around Christmas. Also today, 2 apartment complexes burnt down in Flint. It's my Grandpa's birthday.

Why is it so hard for me to write in my own journal anymore and so easy to write to you? When I had to go to "therapy" I couldn't write anything. Not even the trivial stuff that I write to you. Why, I don't know. Life is truly too weird for me.

When did you stop believing in Santa Claus? I was in 3rd grade. I hope I get a half way decent job in Pittsburgh. I REFUSE to work in a fast food restaurant of any kind. It's too stressful. Maybe I'll get lucky. Such things I have to worry about. Maybe I'll fill this book up with photographs that I'll be taking. I can't see myself filling the whole thing. Perhaps, but not for a while. Tired eyes slowly burning.

22 December 1988
12:25 p.m.

Brian is lying on the floor about 7 inches from the television. Mark is jumping on the couch. I was cleaning. I'm taking a break. If they had the choice, they'd watch fucking television all day! And not semi-educational programs, not even semi-educational game shows, but shit like *The Dating Game* and *The Newlywed Show*. It makes me sick. I was never into that. I quit being into television in 4th or 5th grade and I wasn't addicted. I watched cool stuff like Bugs Bunny and stuff on PBS.

Aww—how sweet. The dogs chewed the wrapping off a present that Mark bought me so Mark looked for it and found it and gave it to me already. It's a little plaque thing that's embroidered and it has a few flowers on it and it says, "I'm glad you're you." Yes, I do feel a little stupid about writing about him being a brat.

I'm getting a manicure today. A gift from my aunt. She met this lady who's into animal rights who gives manicures.

23 December 1988

I got my manicure yesterday. That woman was very interesting…for the town of Flint, you see. She works at this rich place beauty salon. I walked in, and this woman came over to me and asked if I was Jolene, and I said yes, because I am. A few minutes later, this snotty, obese woman looked at me and said, "Who are you with?" and I just looked at her and the manicurist said, "She's with me!" We spent the whole time talking about animals. She said that some woman wanted to put her fur coat on for her, and she wanted to say no, but she just couldn't, so she said, "Do you hear that?" and the woman said, "What?" And she said, "All of those little animals crying." That's funny.

‿✧‿

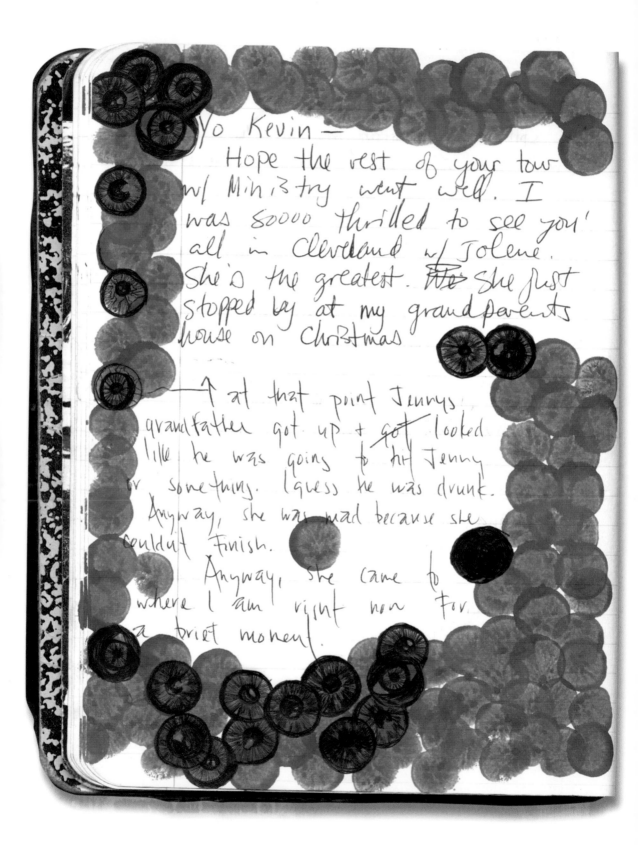

Yo Kevin—
Hope the rest of your tour
w/ Ministry went well. I
was sooooo thrilled to see you
all in Cleveland w/ Jolene.
She's the greatest. ~~The~~ She just
stopped by at my grandparents
house on Christmas

at that point Jennys
grandfather got up + ~~got~~ looked
like he was going to hit Jenny
or something. I guess he was drunk.
Anyway, she was mad because she
couldn't finish.
Anyway, she came to
where I am right now for
a brief moment.

Toledo

I went to a party last night. We were talking about how Jonathon owes me money, and Dawn was saying that I'm too cute to get mad. Oh right! Cute? Why do all of these people think that I'm so sweet? I'm not. I'm hot. I'm wearing a turtleneck. Oh, I'm wearing what I wore at Ministry.

Anyway, these people were saying that I don't look like I could get really angry. The real me is expressed through my right hand. Sad, sad life.

25 December 1988

It's Christmas and I'm very tired. Yesterday I went visiting with my mom. This morning was hell. My mother keeps bitching. Such is life. Excuse me while I take a nap. Merry Christmas.

I'm in the kitchen writing to you. My mom's friend, Rosemary, had this Christmas tree ornament that's a spider web and I loved it. Later on I commented on it and she said that I could have it. It's great. I'm taking it to school.

26 December 1988

Ogre,

Hello. I hope you are well. It's December 26, 1988. I came home (to Flushing) to 10 letters! I felt like you!

I'm not happy, yet I'm very happy, and I'm not really sad but I am quite sad. Sorry. School, you know? I hope '89 is good for you.

Stay well, be good, take care.

Jolene

In the DARKNESS KNOW it WELL Part II

Pittsburgh
1 January 1989

Hi, I'm on my way to Pittsburgh. I look and feel like hell. I slept on my neck wrong and my mother hit me with her curling iron (on purpose) on my elbow. It hurts. She can be such a bitch.

1:44 p.m.—on the road

Hills—lots of hills. We're at some motel in the suburbs of Pittsburgh. Yeah, I'm kind of nervous and my elbow still hurts!

3 January 1989

Get inside. Get inside. The world ends in three days!
—Woman on the street

Well, I'm here at the Art Institute of Pittsburgh. Strange thing. Some girl on my floor came to my door and said, "Do you like Ministry or Skinny Puppy?" and I was like, "What? Why?" and she said, "Because my friend made me this tape of Ministry and Skinny Puppy and I really don't listen to it, so if you want it you can have it." So I invited her in and showed her my photo album. Well, my classes start tomorrow. I better get to sleep. Sweet dreams.

5 January 1989

Hello. I'm at school again but I was back at the dorm. I think my roommate wants a new roommate. She's really conservative and doesn't seem to have any interests.

6:08 p.m.

Blah. Here I am again in a state of depression. Some guy in Pittsburgh was decapitated. Anyway, aside from the fact that I don't think my roommate likes me, some guy grabbed me on the street. I seem to be a little lonely. I met another cool guy today. I wore my conversation piece Skinny Puppy T-shirt.

I'm back. I wonder how you are. I hope you're well. I'm not tired. I'm fucking bored out of my SKULL! Tomorrow is Friday. What's going on? I'm just lying here listening to *The Land of Rape and Honey*.

Hi. I'm at school. It's raining. I fell on the way here.

12:02 a.m.

Sometimes I just want to cry. Not because I'm bored out of my fucking skull—just because.

NO HOPE OF ANYTHING.

Feeling. Feeling sorry that I ever came. I'm depressed.

I went down by the river with this guy in my class. He's nice, though he has an obsession with fires and he'll only date girls into photography. I'm not his type anyway. I'm depressed. Don't yell at me for being down. I'm bored. That's all there is. I'm tired and I want to escape.

7 January 1989
Saturday

Ugh. This guy keeps following me around! He probably thinks I like him because I went to the park with him! I'M FUCKING BORED! I'd rather be dead than bored. I'm so lonely at this moment. My roommate went out. She knows people. Here I am. I know people on the other side of the river. I really, really, really <u>hate</u> this feeling! I've been lonely before, but I've <u>never, ever</u> been so fucking bored in my whole life. FUCK!

8 January 1989
10:14 a.m.

I think I left part of my brain at home! I've done so many brainless things.

Day #1: I locked myself out of my dorm room while at the same time getting my nightshirt caught in the door.

Day #2: I wore my sweater with a pocket on the front <u>backwards</u> for half the day.

Day #5: I lost my ID…looked for it for about an hour. I found it in my footlocker!

I have to go down to "brunch" in a few minutes. Television mind. I don't think my roommate likes me, so I'm going to be quiet all day. So there!

<u>Please leave me alone</u>

That guy keeps following me around. Fuck. It's like, get the hint, guy! I did give him a few hints today. He came over to where I was sitting and he was saying that he got robbed last night and he asked what I did. I said that I didn't do anything and that I like to be alone. UGH. Before I left, he said that he'd call me in an hour and I said that I didn't want to do anything.

You want 2. He wants 3. They want 4.

I'm bored.

13 January 1989
Friday
10:46 p.m.

Hello. I'm tired and I'd really love to go to sleep but there are 3 guys outside my door and Joe left his keys in here, so I can't really fall asleep. He seems to be afraid of me. He thinks I'm evil or something. Which I am not.

I'm going to a party. I'm supposed to go to Bryant's but he lives on the North side. It's dangerous over there.

11:48 p.m.

Blah fuck.

I went to a very boring party where I felt so out of place I could have died. My stomach hurts. Some guy named Dale brought me home. Sorry. Bye.

Bryant

23 cuts on my wrist and all is well. Oh dear. Where shall I start? Well, Bryant, Elizabeth, Gyllian and I went to the zoo. It was fun. At about 6:00, I ventured out alone, taking the bus to the Allegheny Apartments. I got Lisa and we went up to Bryant's at about 9:30 and drank beer. There were a bunch of people there. I was hanging out in Bryant's room with Art (his roommate) and Bryant came in and gave me a massage and then I gave him one. He went into the other room because he heard a big crash so I went out, and I swear it hadn't even been 2 minutes since we were in the bedroom and this girl went up to him and attacked him. I was like "fine," so I just went over in the other room with Phoebe, Marc, Dickie, and Al. I picked up Bryant's exacto knife and started cutting my wrist. Phoebe said, "No, I won't let you." But I didn't want to cut my wrist to die or anything so I just kept doing it. She picked up a blade and started cutting her arm and she was drinking her blood. Bryant came over and looked at me, then looked at my wrist and licked it. Then Dickie grabbed my knife and started hacking away at his wrist and his cuts were really deep and he was tripping on acid and he was not well. Then some asshole was saying racial things to this black guy Bullwinkle and he said, "I'll kick your ass" and the guy said, "I don't care, kick my ass" and Bullwinkle said, "I won't kick your ass, I'll fucking kill you. I'll shoot you and I'll slit your neck." He left and said he'd be back so we left. Strange.

23 January 1989

Ogre,

Salvador Dali died. I worry about your wellbeing, Ogre. Honestly and sincerely. Some screwy shit is going on and I don't understand.

5 February 1989
4:15 p.m.

Last night we invited people to our dorm. Lisa also came to visit. We decided we wanted to drink. Ugh. It all happened pretty fast. The next thing I knew, Lisa told Aaron that we'd give him a full body massage. Aaron told Steve to leave. That's when things got fucked up. Aaron started kissing me. I was falling asleep and all these things were being done to me, then I suddenly felt sick. I ran into the bathroom and got sick and sick and sick. I came back into the room and he was kissing Lisa, then she sat on the floor and he was kissing me again and he said, "Are we gonna screw or what?" I was pissed. I went back into the bathroom and got sick again. I came back into the room and got under the covers and passed out. That was my evening. At lunch, Lisa and I were in the cafeteria and Aaron walked by and said, "Hi, girls." I felt like saying, "You asshole!" but I refrained.

9:26 p.m.

I have this tremendous urge to cut myself, but for one thing, my roommate would freak out, and fucking Aaron took my razor blade. He's such an asshole.

I will probably see Bryant tomorrow. Who knows what's going on. I saw Aaron this morning before breakfast. He was like, "Hi, Jolene," and I was like, "Fuck off." True, he is hot, but arrogant. There are some things I cannot say.

7 February 1989

Happy Birthday, Grandma. Bless her soul. I saw Aaron this morning. He went out of his way to say hello. He pays more attention to me now than he did before. Crazy. Anyway, who cares? I worked all day, then went to the lab. I saw Bryant. He was happy to see me. I really should go before I fall asleep.

8:58 p.m.

Hello, I'm about to walk to the Greyhound station with Brad and Kim and possibly Jeff. La la. I'm listening to Clan of Xymox. I called Lindy collect. For some reason she asked me if I'm still writing to you. Of course. Ouch. Actually, itch. I cut my little wrist once again.

Bryant wasn't at school today so I couldn't ignore his slut self. Oh well, I guess I have to accept the fact that he's slept with a jock chick. I can proudly say that I'm probably the most cultured person he's ever gone out with. Jock chick. Give me a break. Have you ever gone out with a jock chick? Well, I guess Bryant is the most conservative guy I've gone out with.

i care too much.

HAPPY VALENTINES DAY... 2 YEARS WRITING

Hello- A day when affection
is accepted.
Anyway, I'm sorry that I'm
not demented & funny anymore.
I don't understand it myself — but
I know that 2 years ago I bought
REMISSION & so began the
abstract letters from
yours truly.
          Its all worth it you know
very much worth it
take care —
be Good —
smile.
♡ JOLENE

16 February 1989
9:35 p.m.

How is your life? Mine is ever so confusing. Ugh. I met this guy, Jason, who is into Skinny Puppy. He's really hot and I've been wanting to know him for quite some time. He said that I have marshmallow white skin.

18 February 1989
10:42 p.m.

Q: How does one make another jealous?
A: Sleep with his roommate.

Hello. Life is certainly funny. We went to Allegheny Center and ended up going over to Al's apartment to drink. I fell asleep at about 11 p.m. because I'd been up since 6:45 a.m. They were watching these stupid porn flicks. At 11:30 we were supposed to go to #707. Bryant lives at #705 and I thought I'd run into him. But I didn't. I did see Art, his roommate. We went into #708 and we were drinking their beer and we went into the bathroom and everyone was getting high. As the night progressed Art, Kim (my roommate), and I went to Lisa's apartment and Art and I gave each other a massage with Lisa's toy spider. It was fun. Then we played with her stuffed animals.

This stupid hick was hitting on Kim so we went to Art's room and this girl Shannon that likes him stopped by and he was annoyed. It was about 3 a.m. and we decided that we were going to stay at Art's and Bryant's. Kim slept on the couch and Art and I sat on the mattress talking and listening to music. He's so sweet. We also relaxed each other by massages. We talked about so much and it was really cool. I didn't fall asleep until about 6 a.m. or so.

At about 11 a.m. I heard Bryant and his girlfriend talking. I wondered what he'd think when he saw me lying next to Art in his bed. After about a half-hour of hearing Bryant and his jock chick girlfriend May laughing, Bryant came out. I was sleeping with the blanket over my head and I felt someone's presence right over me. Then he lifted the cover from my head and it scared me and I looked at him and his expression was priceless! He said, "Oh, I wondered who that was!" And I just looked at him and he said, "Hi" and I said, "Hi" and I pulled the

covers back over my head. It was SO hilarious. He went back into the bedroom and they were really quiet.

22 February 1989
10:09 p.m.

Well, I've been busy and content lately. Last night Kim, Jack, and I modeled. It was so much fun. Jack is such a sweetheart. When am I going to finish this book? Be good to your ever so intelligent self.

Jolene

It makes me sad. I'm sure you don't appreciate me telling you this, but…I hardly know you, but I really care about you. I don't know if…I don't know. It's not a fantasy. Honestly, it's not. I care about you as a person. I don't have dreams about having sex with you or anything typical like that. I just look up to you. You're such a nice person. I was a little upset when you said, "Your problems aren't my problems," I think you understand that I just need an outlet. It helps me to write how I feel and send it off. It helps me. I know you don't read the whole content of my books and I understand.

25 February 1989

Talk about depressing days. That was yesterday and it was because I listened to stuff like Simon and Garfunkel and Joy Division.

Jack, Kim & Jeff
Jack

Also, I was depressed and still am because I talked to my aunt and I was telling her that my mom thinks that I'm spending money on dumb things and I'm not. I'm just upset because I'm trying really hard and I don't even know if I'll have enough money to come here next quarter, and there are people like my friend Michelle who can go out and buy new clothes every week and still have tuition money. The worst part about it is that she misses a lot of classes and when she does decide to come she comes in late. Upsetting.

12 March 1989

It's been a while. I've just been so busy. It doesn't really matter. It's 4:37 p.m. on a Sunday afternoon and I'm listening to Christian Death. Well, I'm in an all right state of mind at the moment. I've been studying.

3:15 p.m.

I'm on my way to Cleveland. I'm going to Tracy's. Remember Tracy? I met her when you played Columbus in 1987. Anyway, tomorrow she's going to Toledo with me. Actually, I don't feel like writing now. See you later.

～～

19 March 1989
Sunday

Hello. I'm in Toledo in my old bedroom. Scary. I just read some pages from a diary I had 3 years ago. It's wild. I'm going away with my mother today. She's into basketball. That's scary.

I like Pittsburgh better than Toledo. Is my writing hard to read? I do apologize if it is. I'm so very tired. I really wish I would finish this book. I am so busy at school, therefore this section may or may not be interesting. I'm just not as demented as I used to be.

～～

My mom owes money. Money money money. I <u>will</u> become a good photographer. Who knows, perhaps I'll get into films. All I know is that I'm going to do my best and use my money wisely. I'm going to travel and have lots of fun.

Have I gone and turned positive on you? Yes, I think that's what has happened. I'm still paranoid about death and sometimes I give too much of myself away, but I have learned <u>not</u> to trust people. I am looking out for <u>me</u> and that's how I want it to be. I am nice to people but I have to look out for me to keep myself alert so that I don't screw up and get taken advantage of. I am important, to me anyway, and if I can save myself from hurt and from being a victim to whatever, that is what I will do, because once I start my career, no one is going to take care of me and watch over me and there are people out there who look for people who are vulnerable and I'm just not going to fall into that.

There is truth to "Life is what you make it," and I don't even need chemicals.

～～

My aunt is going to pay for my schooling. My mother is poor at the moment, though she's going to Hawaii in May.

～～

12:00 a.m.

Hello. I'm still in Toledo. My mother is getting on my nerves. I mean, I don't hate the person that she is, but I am everything that she's not. I'm not saying that I'm better than her, but I don't know. She does not budget her money. I do. She drinks every day (just about). I really don't mind being drunk though I really don't like the taste of beer. And with alcohol I know when to stop. I don't know. Life is strange and for this very second of this day during this year I suppose I like myself. I wish she would go to bed. She's smoking a cigarette. Tell me why she gets so fucking stubborn when she's drunk. What's the point? Please grow up, mother. Why do I waste my time writing to you? You flat out told me you won't write. What's my problem?

Ugh. My mom went to bed.

30 March 1989

Hello. Gee, it's been awhile. I'm truly sorry, though I'm quite sure you didn't miss me. Anyway, I'm back in Pittsburgh and I'm in a relatively good mood. I don't know. It seems like I'm always busy though.

8 April 1989

OK, so I'm depressed and it's not a selfish depression. My mother came to Pittsburgh to see a basketball game. I was going to a party last night, and I had already told her that I had plans so I had to leave her early. I felt bad because she had an hour or so until the game started.

Today, Saturday, I took her down to the Strip District (by the Metropol) and I could tell she wasn't thrilled by it. I directed her to Oakland (where Graffiti is) and we couldn't find a parking place, so I took her to Station Square and we looked around and got a salad. There was nothing else to do so

JOLENE Box 426
Point Park College 201 Wood St.
Pittsburgh, PA 15222-1983
USA

Is Evil
something you are
or something you do?

What is
Happiness?

PHOTOS
ENCLOSED

to: KEVIN OGILVIE
c/o NETTWERK
BOX 330
1755 Robson St.
Vancouver, BC
V6G-3B7
Canada

my mother was going back to her hotel. I wondered if she was mad because there was nothing to do. She was not mad. I asked her if she was sad and she said she was sort of sad because she shouldn't have come to Pittsburgh because of her car. I agree. She forgot to give me the $8.

11:39 p.m.

You wouldn't believe the shit going on now. So, I cut deeper. Little, stupid, trivial things can get so fucked. Wrist blood looks pink.

So, get this. Joe approached Andrea and told her that he thinks I need HELP. What the fuck. Do I really? I may or may not have said before that I used to think it was cool to be depressed, but I don't think it's cool anymore. Yet I am and my friends say I need help.

My mother once said, "You have no idea how many people care about you." Andrea said the same tonight. If all of these people care about me so much, then why the fuck don't I feel it? Andrea said she's envious because I decorate my envelopes. Big fucking deal. It's not going to get me anywhere in life.

22 April 1989
Afternoon
Market Square

I join the weirdoes. I am sitting here on a bench next to a man who is having a conversation with no one in sight.

He's talking about money and his own business. Pretty strange. My scalp is baking in this hot sun, but the wind is cool so that's OK. Perhaps he's talking to the pigeons.

I came out alone today, because I really need to be alone, away from the dorms. Now there is a man behind me who is singing joyfully aloud. This is kind of fun. I just hope I don't get a tan. Lucky you. Every year at this time you get to hear about how much I hate tans. I do. In a big way.

29 April 1989
12:26 p.m.

Lately I've been thinking about the incomplete part of me. I mean, I have no idea who my father is. There is another half of me that I don't know anything about.

What does he look like? In what ways do I look like him? Is he a really gross bum? He was an exchange student from Bogota, Columbia. That's so incredibly weird that I am really half Colombian. And I do believe I look that way. Actually, I'm not really sure if he's from Bogota, but I know it's somewhere in South America.

Did I tell you that I have a half-sister? I don't know her. See, my mother gave her up for adoption. She's 2 years older than me. I want to know about my other half. It confuses me so.

Jolene _____ / Ph / 2A
Student Name   Dept.   Qtr./Sect.

Please come to the <u>Counseling and Housing Services Office</u> on:

Date: Tues. April 18   Time: 1:30   *

Your Appointment is with:

✓ Counselor Karen Uhrin _____
___ Readmissions Advisor _____
___ Student Services Systems Coordinator _____
___ Director of Housing Services _____
___ Director of Student Services _____

The Counseling and Housing Services Office is located in the
mezzanine area on the second floor.

*Should this time be inconvenient for you, please stop
by so that we can arrange a more suitable time.

May 1989

Ogre,

Hello dear.

Life is so fucking pleasant. I'm tired, but before I rest I shall inform you that I freaked out my roommate Andrea by cutting my wrist, and she told the head of counseling and I'm supposedly going to be ordered to get counseling from Point Park College (where the dorms are) and the Art Institute of Pittsburgh. Andrea moved out.

NEXT DAY

I saw Andrea at breakfast and she said hi to me. I don't understand. This morning the school counselor called me down and she said that people are concerned because I tried to take my life. Correction. I did NOT try to take my life. She wants me to start going down to see her regularly, which is all right with me. Past experiences with counselors have been OK.

Anyway, I asked that my mother NOT find out. She said I should speak to John Hupp (dorm guy) before he calls my mother. If my mother finds out, she's going to freak out! She'll be so disappointed because she thinks I'm so happy here, which I was…

8 May 1989
5:29 p.m.

Hello. This girl Bev is coming over later with acid. I have never done acid. This should be pretty cool. Adam and Jack and Bev will also be doing acid. I'm pretty nervous. I'm only doing this because I want to be more creative and I've been reading about LSD. We're doing it at 6. I've been excited all day. I'm going to do a drawing or something for you. Anticipation. I'm painting my nails. Lindy just called and, well, I just couldn't tell her about it.

6:22 p.m.

Well, there's no turning back now. Now all I have to do is wait. We're listening to *Mind: TPI.*

6:35 p.m.

I'm still waiting.

6:47 p.m.

Gee whiz. This arm feels kind of weird and Adam is telling me what to do. Like my fears.

7:36 p.m.

Kind of vulnerable and weird.

7:40 p.m.

My aunt called and she doesn't know what I'm doing. It feels like before.

8:37 p.m.

It's all like I'm back in time. I feel my foot sliding.

They are all cool.

8:42 p.m.

Too weird. Crawling.

It's teeth.

I like this.

I wrote that. This is really cool. It just feels really nice right now.

Maybe I'll do this again. Wow. Nerves and stuff.

It's just really tight in my neck, but I like it a lot.

So nice in my hands.

I understand.

I think everything is pretty. Everything is surprising me.

I don't want to look at skin.

11:39 a.m.

I think I'm starting to come down but I still like it.

12:04 a.m.

It's still pretty weird.

Things still look weird. I can still feel my whole body. It's so intense. I feel everything.

It's rather strange. I feel my brain and my fingers and my hair.

I feel my stomach.

This is so weird.

It's 1:28 a.m. and Jack and I are just hanging out. I could hear everything.

AWARE

AWARENESS

WARM FUZZIES. COLD PDICKIELES.

3:47 a.m.

Still?

It's weirding me out. Glass houses. Oops.

9 May 1989

Lindy,

PLEASE DON'T TELL ANYONE.

      Hell O.

      Well, I have to tell you something and I know that you will be completely through LSD eyes.

LSD eyes
to look

my arm

12-

He
l d
sayi
nice
head
doesnt

disappointed in me. I'm going to try to explain something. Lately things are really strange and I don't even care. It's like I'm lost or something. I felt like I needed an outlet so I got high last weekend. It didn't make me feel great and I didn't forget reality. Then I thought I really wanted to be creative and I've been hearing about acid. Jack has been telling me a lot and I started thinking about it because last week Ian was putting down drugs and Aaron said, "How can you put drugs down when you don't even do them? I read all about LSD and I heard all these cool stories about tripping and hallucinating so I thought I'd want to try it. I told Jack and he asked this hippy girl, Bev, if she had any acid and she said she was going to get some.

We planned to do it on Tuesday night because I didn't have anything to do today. I thought it was a sign from someone, when you called, that I shouldn't do it. But at 6 I put the paper on my tongue, let it get soggy and then swallowed it. It's so bizarre. Your perception of reality is so weird. I just wanted to see how Ogre feels and I wanted to be creative.

Jack, Bev, Vince, and I did it. Tripping is definitely the word for it. You think <u>so</u> much. I can't believe I did it. See, when you do it you have to be totally comfortable and in a good mood. Your surroundings have to be nice too. LSD makes you paranoid. <u>Please</u> don't tell your mom, because I'm afraid she won't let you hang out with me. I'm also afraid that she'd tell my mom. Anyway, I don't think I'll do it again. It made my neck really tense and my stomach sort of hurt when I was coming down. I made a really cool painting.

I would never do anything else. As a matter of fact, at about 4 this morning, I decided that I don't want to drink, smoke pot, or anything. You think so much. You're like conscious above consciousness.

It felt like a movie and a dream. Everything had meaning. When I saw my wrists bleeding I was freaking. I can see how people totally freak. You just forget what it's like to be sane and it's sort of scary.

I'm sort of worried about myself because 1½ weeks ago I was <u>so</u> against drugs. I know, I'm stupid, but I did it for the experience. It's over now. You can lecture me. I actually wouldn't mind, because maybe I'd feel like someone still cares about me. I wish I could come home for a weekend. I need to get away from here. Perhaps tripping was a bad way to escape. I just need to get back to my old life for a while. I miss it. I don't know. I'm sure you're disappointed. I hope you are. I knew if I told you when you called that I was going to do acid, that you'd be able to talk me out of it. This past week has been just too weird for me. I can't handle it, obviously. I should go.

Write soon.

Jolene

piss fuck head.

17 May 1989
Ogre,

Hello. I'm at school. And I'm having a hard time coping. I can truly understand why people do drugs. I don't think I'll do anything besides acid. It was such an escape. I need something. I really feel awful that Jack is doing drugs again. It's my fault for wanting to do them.

How many times have you done acid? After 7 times or so, you're legally psychotic. What if you're already psychotic and you do acid 7 times? Jack has done it 51 times. I told him to imagine doing it, being in that state of mind for 51 days. The only thing about acid that scares me is having to worry about flashbacks. This fat teacher is such an asshole. I can't stand him. I can't stand this babbling wobbly teacher!

20 May 1989
6:25 p.m.
Market Square
Ogre,

Well, here I am with Bev, Adam, and Jack. Bev and Bev took acid around 2 p.m. and Jack and I just did at 6 p.m. Anyway, we're waiting. The wider the aperture, the less depth of field. I'm trying to get a hold of my mom. Well, she wasn't home. Jack is calling his father. It's hot and I'm starting to feel tension in my neck.

7:00 p.m.

Jack seems to be disturbed.

7:04 p.m.

At Market Square, some old man in a yellow shirt riding a bike tried to pick me up. Ali is sober and she's here with all of us who aren't.

7:26 p.m.

Everything is peaceful. I like acid a lot. A LOT. I'm feeling it a lot now. Jack is being apathetic. Everything is warm. Why can't the world be like this all the time? Bev is writing, Bev is drawing, and Jack is drawing. Ali is writing.

7:39 p.m.

Ali left.

8:04 p.m.

Things are pretty strange. I'm laughing at myself again because my scars were getting darker. It's very light here in my room. Crush the spine. This drug is just too cool. My walls are definitely breathing. I have to go to the bathroom. I hope I don't see anything too strange. I'm looking at your picture and your face is going to explode.

8:19 p.m.

I feel small.

8:23 p.m.

Yes, I'm tripping. I'm listening to my headphones. *Vivisect VI*. It couldn't sound any better than this. I'm watching my walls. In this trip I'm a little more introverted. And I'm used to what's happening to my skin. I'm enjoying this immensely. Wow. Lindy called me the other night and bitched me out for doing acid. I'm being swallowed up by this music. I like acid and I'm glad that Lindy cares but this is fun and she's never done it.

9:15 p.m.

We're down in Adam's room now. Everyone is just hanging out. Jack asked me if I'm OK. Yes, I'm OK. I'm tripping, remember? I'm trying to write neatly. I feel all wet. I'm just watching everything.

We're going to taste an apple. It's just an apple. Our apple experience. A good apple. This texture and taste. It's pretty wild. The best apple I've ever had. Adam was freaking out because I'm tripping. I just sold Yvonne's hit.

No time to see reality.

11:40 p.m.

Well. I'm hanging out here in my room with Jack. It is blue. Everything. The mood is blue because I have a blue light on and I just realized that I can't see the blue lines on this paper. Fuck it. I'm not going to try to write neat anymore.

12:19 p.m.

The beauty of no music. The beauty of not wearing makeup. The beauty of lying here in my blue little bed, tripping and watching the world through LSD eyes.

Jack is biting my arm.

12:42 p.m.

He's still biting my arm. He could bite right into it. I'm wearing headphones. Jack said he doesn't mind. PRIZEWORK.

I sold Adam Yvonne's hit and I made a $1.50 profit. Ogre, I idolize you.

I'm sorry that little, demented, tripping Jolene idolizes you, but your lyrics...Just you. I idolize you. Acid. Acid. This trip isn't as intense as the first but it's a trip all the same and being here in my blue little world I'm wishing that I could talk to you. Jack is sucking my index toe. He said he could bite it off. Jack is strange and he's still sucking my toes. Ugh. My stomach hurts.

21 May 1989
1:00 p.m.

Jack and I are in Burger King and I am drinking ice water. Jack and I are just kind of mellow right now. I have to take pictures but I am so tired.

After 2 or so

Jack and I are sitting in a very peaceful, very small cemetery. It is nice. We're just thinking about acid and how to trip without taking it.

I like the way the sun is falling through the leaves. It's flickering little circles of sunshine. It's nice here in the shade, watching the world through sane eyes. Taking it all in as if I were on LSD. I wonder if it would look better if I were on the drug. I'm convincing myself that it is perfect and that it can't look any better. I wonder how you look at the world.

You've taken so much. Is it old yet? John Lennon had over 1000 trips and his kids turned out all right. Are you going to have kids? Do you like tripping?

We're sitting next to a tomb of an Indian. His name was Mio-Qua-Coo-Na-Caw or "Red Pole." Principal Village Chief of the Shawnee Nation. He died in Pittsburgh on January 28, 1797. That was a long time ago.

Why do we need drugs? Why does anyone need drugs? The Adam that I sold a hit to last night trips just to feel weird. I do it for the experience. I do artwork and I write. That's why and you know what? I like it.

Jack is meditating. We're pretty down. We'll probably leave soon. The gum I'm chewing is pretty gross and my right foot has fallen asleep.

22 May 1989
Monday

Jack and I decided that we don't need drugs to be creative. Luckily my second trip wasn't very good. I honestly don't know what made me try the drug in the first place. I don't want to get messed up. You understand, don't you?

I'm having a hard time here because I feel that there is only one person here that I can talk to, and even then we don't always agree. You know the kind of people that I really cannot stand? People that go out and lie in the sun all day and then flaunt their suntan as if they're really talented. How much effort does it take to go and be lazy? Oh well, I laugh at them because I KNOW. What do I know? Well, I know that I'm not going to have skin cancer and I'm doing more constructive things with my time and well, you know how it is.

My mother is going to Hawaii tomorrow. She earned a trip by selling this Christmas merchandise. I hope her trip goes well. I am totally jealous of anyone who gets to travel. I love going places. I'm jealous of bands. You're lucky you get to go all over the place and people are glad to see you. It seems like it would be a completely comfortable adventure. Maybe someday I'll be rich and I'll be able to travel. I lost $5 and I'm not happy about it.

24 May 1989
6:00 p.m.

Hello, Jack and I just took a bus to Oakland (outside of Pittsburgh) and walked 3 million miles to this place called the Electric Banana. My throat hurts in a big way. Birds are chirping. We're waiting for this band ALL to get here.

Hey, one of my instructors says that I'm a good student. He said yesterday that I am one of the best students and today he told me twice that I am a good student. You don't understand (well, you might) how much that means to me. I guess maybe since I blew off the University of Toledo that I learned my lesson. I am proud of myself. I think I'm growing up. Scary thought.

I wondered if Bill from ALL remembered me from the time I hung out with the band last year. Bill is the drummer. He said that he did and that's why he kept looking at me, and he said that I used to wear my hair "more radical" and I used to look more like death. Totally death. I suppose that's another sign of growing up. Well, the show is about to begin.

Jack & ME

25 May 1989

I saw ALL last night. They put me on the guest list. They all remembered me! Gooch isn't with them anymore though. It was pretty cool. Dickie is buying me a personal pan pizza for lunch.

26 May 1989

All I can think about anymore is tripping. It's scaring me. I guess I'll get drunk tonight. Reality is treating me fine. I just like euphoria.

10:10 p.m.

Well, I'm drinking but I wish I were tripping. All I keep thinking about is acid. Adam and I are hanging out watching these people from CBS filming a "Movie of the Week." I bet we look strange, sitting here on the ground. That's OK though.

1:23 a.m.

Well, here I am alone in my room listening to The Cult. Anyway, Jack is out with his friends from Ft. Wayne. He'd better not be getting high. He's supposed to stop. If he's tripping I'll be really upset because I wish I were. I can't understand why ALL I ever think about lately is tripping. It's just too much fun.

2:07 a.m.

I'm so so tired I could collapse. Perhaps if I force myself to stay up I'll hallucinate.

27 May 1989
Saturday

I will refrain for the time being. VICES. Do you understand? I had the most amazing fun each time I tripped. I do feel the need to speak to someone sane. I want to talk to you. YES, I'm still happy. I haven't been sad lately, just a little confused. I'm going to drink tonight just for something to do. I'm going through the strangest self-destructive phase of my life. My roommate Kim is REALLY getting on my nerves. I don't care. I'm not letting her know that she bothers me. I know she's dying to hear me complain about her bad attitude but GUESS WHAT? I'm not going to. Her way is going to get back at her in the end. I will be happy and content. What do you think about my philosophy? I like it. I believe in it.

29 May 1989
8:49 p.m.

Well, I get to come home in about 2 weeks. If things go as planned, Tiffany is going to drive to Toronto. I want to spend a long time there, but my money situation is just not good!

My roommate Kim is being a materialistic bitch. She has this really bad attitude. She's so rude that she has unplugged her TV and set it on the floor so I can't watch it. I miss David Letterman. She's in visual communications and I draw better that her. I've been talking about her a lot lately, but her way is really getting to me! I mean, I wonder about society. You're supposedly in good hands if you have a mother and father in the same household and you're well off. The thing is, it seems to me that most of the above-average intelligent people are either not well off or are raised by divorced parents, etc. Kim has the "All-American Family," but she's so empty. She just exists and she has nothing of any importance to show for her life.

Anyway, despite all of the problems my mother and I have had, I think she raised me pretty well. I suppose I should tell her that.

I just cried about my grandparents. I miss them so much. Oh well, life goes on. Well, I'd better be going. If you have time, write me.

Take care,

Jolene

3 June 1989
4:30 p.m. (scary coincidence)

Ogre,

I need to write to you at this moment more than I ever had to. Early this morning, at 4:30 a.m. to be exact, I got a double ring (out of the building) call. At first I had a hard time understanding who it was because he was mumbling. Anyway, it was Dickie and he sounded wasted. He asked if he could come over, but I had to say that he couldn't because I can't have guests after 1 a.m. He was crying hysterically, saying that he wanted to kill himself. I asked him where he was and he said he was at his apartment. He was alone. I got off the phone, got dressed, and Jack and I went downstairs. I was so nervous. Finally Dickie arrived. He parked his car and threw his keys, then he staggered, ran, and hugged me. Then he banged his head against the wall. I was terrified. He sat down and I sat down with him and he hugged me. I looked at his arms and he had carved HATE DEATH HATE in huge letters and on the other arm he wrote HATE. On his right arm he also had 3 cigarette burns right on the veins in his wrist.

I started freaking out. He was screaming, "I want to fucking die!" I didn't know what to do. A few times, he said he couldn't breathe. I thought he was going to choke. All I could think to do was to tell him to breathe slowly and deeply. I was so scared. I thought I should call someone but I didn't know who. Dickie was screaming, "I'm a lunatic." He said he needed a cigarette and I was trying to light it for him and he tried burning his wrist again. I was scared. I yelled at him and told him that I wouldn't let him. He threw his shoes. Some people walked by and Dickie screamed, "Jolene, just kill me." I almost freaked out. I said, "No, Dickie I'm not going to kill you. You called me at 4:30 in the morning for help. I care and I'm helping you." He would freak out, then apologize saying, "Jolene, you're so cool. You're the only one who can understand me." He also kept saying, "I love you, you're my best friend." But then he would freak out again. He pulled chunks of his hair out. I had to grab his hand away. Once I was hugging him and he went to pull his hair out and my hair was hanging over his and he pulled on my hair. I was scared that he was going to hurt me. He kept saying, "I'm sorry, Jolene, I'm so sorry." I told him not to be sorry and that I'm glad he called me, which I am. He said he was driving (highly intoxicated) and he saw this cop and he stopped and said, "I need help," and the cop said, "You're crazy." He threw his cigarettes, matches, and anything he held. He talked about his parents, girls, school, and his job. I didn't know how to handle it, but I did and that's what counts.

6 June 1989
1:05 p.m.

Well, I saw Dickie today. He seemed to be all right. He didn't say anything about the other night. Anyway, I'm having strange feelings lately. I'm going out with Jack. He said that he loves me, but that's so scary. I leave Pittsburgh on Friday. Summer break.

10 June 1989
12:24 a.m.

Hey, I'm in Toledo and I'm 20 because today is my birthday and I'm drinking with Lindy and that's cool. I miss Jackolantern Jack. He's a sweetheart. Dickie phoned me Thursday night. He was in the hospital. I phoned him today and the man at the hospital said that he left the hospital yesterday with a pass and he was supposed to return but he never did. So, I have to worry. I miss Jack. Lindy is tipsy.

⌐⌐

Life is truly confusing. I thought confusion ended with adolescence. I suppose not. Another problem I have to deal with is money. Always money. The lack of money, that is. Money for school, money for everything. Jack bought me flowers yesterday. How did life find me? I would like to know.

12 June 1989
Monday

Here I am at 1:03 a.m. and still confused. So, Jack wants me to do acid again when I get back to Pittsburgh. I want to, but I don't want to get addicted. Why do I need this escape? I'm not depressed—deeply depressed, that is, but my experience was so great.

13 June 1989
9:24 p.m.

I know this letter must be very confusing to you. I'm so alone this moment. It reminds me so much of how it was when I was living here in Toledo. Depression. Nothing to do. No one to talk to.

I'm bored out of my skull! Jack said he'd call me at 9 p.m. and it's already 9:24. Boredom. Bored. Bored. My mother is at a friend's and I have no car to drive.

10:24 p.m.

Jack still hasn't called. I do hate being here alone, especially since I had a horrible nightmare last night. I don't even have a bedroom here. My mother has converted my room into some sort of junk room.

I'm sighing at the thought of my past. I do love being on my own. I was so lost and alone here in Toledo. I think that moving to Pittsburgh is the best thing I could've done. I have grown up so much. I truly love my mother and I admire her for raising me, but I simply cannot live with her.

15 June 1989
1:06 a.m.

Not even 24 hours left in Toledo. I'm going to Lima tomorrow, then Fort Wayne on Friday. Jack lives in Fort Wayne.

2:30 p.m.

UGH. I'm leaving today and everything is SO unorganized. I truly hate being unorganized. I called Greyhound and a round trip ticket is like 30-some dollars!! Oh, excuse me. I just spilled iced tea on this letter.

❧

Jack had some pot and I was upset because he promised himself that he wouldn't get high anymore, but he bought it and I didn't want him to do it with his friends so I did it with him. I got really messed up. Doesn't anyone care anymore? I don't know why I'm asking you. I'm sorry.

Jack's mom has invited me to stay with them all next week. That's really sweet. I don't want everyone to think that my mother's such a bad mother, because she's not. We just have a really strange relationship. She's just moody. Why is life so confusing?

16 June 1989
1:00 a.m. or so

Tiffany and I are at Andy and Sean's. I've had a nice weekend. Seeing Jack was pretty cool. His mom made us a really great vegetarian dinner and in the evening we hung out with strange people and then went to see the Rocky Horror Picture Show. We got high. I really wasn't planning on it, but he had it so I figured I would. We fell asleep at the movie, then we went to this all-night restaurant, then we got high again in the car and again when we got back to Jack's. I was so messed up. I have never been so high in my life but I had a great time.

Saturday was pretty strange. We hung out. We went to the cemetery and took great photos then we got high and watched movies. I had to say goodbye to Jack. He's a really sweet guy.

19 June 1989
12:30 a.m.

I AM DEPRESSED.

I'm in Flushing, Michigan, at my aunt's house. I am depressed because I'm convinced that my mother really didn't want me to come home. I know she loves me, but she had all of her junk in "my bedroom," and therefore I ended up sleeping on the living room floor because she didn't want me to sleep on the couch. Anyway, not like this is important but she had absolutely no food and she really didn't want to give me money to eat. Would you feel wanted? I mean, I know she's low on money, but I felt like she just really didn't want me there. It's just depressing, you know? I spent the weekend in Fort Wayne and Lima.

4 July 1989

Hello. It's approximately 8 a.m. About a half an hour ago, my mother disowned me. I am on a Greyhound bus in the very front seat and I am sharing it with a young boy who would rather not be sitting near me. I feel really numb right now. I can't even believe how numb I feel.

At 7 a.m. this morning Lindy phoned me to tell me that Kurt (from Information Society) called her last night. Anyway, OK, my feelings are coming back and I'm about to cry. My "mother" started screaming at me because she had to take me to the bus station. So I got off the phone and started getting ready. I asked her if she'd stop at 7-11 so that I could get something for breakfast. I put my hat on so that I wouldn't have to carry it and she started yelling, "You look like a fucking freak with that hat on and I won't take you to the store if you wear that hat." So she helped me carry one single bag. I'm lucky at that. I got in the car and she started screaming at me (by the way, there are a bunch of dead, smashed flies on the window). She started saying how ugly I am and how I dress like a "sleaze" and how she doesn't even want me to come home again and that she's going to move and no one will know where she is and that she's not going to pay her $50 a month loan (for my school) and that I'm nothing and ugly and evil and that I'm a Satanist. The truth of the whole fucking thing is that SHE is the evil one. She has made me insecure and made me feel that I'm worthless. I keep trying to tell myself that she's wrong so that I won't cry or get depressed. She really does hate me and I don't understand why.

She said that I embarrass her and that most parents can be proud of their children. The fact is that she should be proud of me. I'm actually doing something with my life. When she was 20, she got pregnant by a South American exchange student and she had to give her up for adoption. At 22 she got pregnant in the exact same manner and fought to keep me. My "father" doesn't even know I exist. I'm doing well in school. My mother says that I'm stupid, but I like to think that I'm not. I'm not, am I? As soon as I got to the station she said that she hated me and she wouldn't help me. So I got inside, bought my ticket and sat down. All of the people there were staring at me and I wanted so badly to cry.

Anyway, my bus came and some bad-smelling bum came over and offered to carry my heaviest bag. I let him and when he was carrying it his body swayed to one side and I thought he was going to fall over. He asked if I had bricks in there. When he put my luggage down he leaned against a pole and looked at me with these glassy, watery, stoned eyes and said, "Give me a kiss." I said, "I can't kiss you," and he asked, "Why not?" I said, "My boyfriend would get jealous." He said, "I'll kick his ass," and I said, "He's big!" and he said, "I'll kick his ass anyway." So much for that. Then I leaned against the wall and for a moment suicide flashed through my twisted, tormented brain, but I thought it would only satisfy her, and besides, I don't want to die.

I wish I could wake up some morning and be someone else. Someone perfect. But no one is perfect and am I really that bad? Would my mother be satisfied if I wore pastel colors 7 days a week and had a tan? Surely she would find a flaw in me. She always has. I hate her. I do! I've had 2 dreams in the last 3 weeks that she died and I cried hysterically. I don't know if I would now. But what can I do? Grant her every wish and be her Barbie doll? No. Not quite. She's an alcoholic. She's a beautician with no life insurance and no benefits and she's getting burned out. She needs help. I'm sorry that I have to bore you with this. Honestly, I'm not being overly dramatic or anything. I'm telling the truth. It's fresh in my mind and I have to get rid of it. Here I am. Numb again. You wouldn't believe how cool the rain on the window looks. No, I'm not on drugs. It really does look cool.

10:00 a.m.

I'm in the Cleveland Greyhound bus stop. I just phoned Tracy and she is on her way. She is a good friend of mine. Good long-distance friend, that is, and now she will be going to my school and she will be my roommate. I've known her for a little over 2 years. I hope we will get along. Greyhound busses are dreadful. My hands are sore from carrying my 3-ton duffel bag. Anyway, I'm sitting on it at the moment and it makes a comfortable chair.

Tracy

175

12 July 1989

Yesterday, an obviously homeless old man came into the place where I work and set 4 pieces of candy on my register. I looked at him and he smiled and winked at me. Then I thought to myself, "What a sweet thing that was," even though I knew that I wouldn't eat the candy.

He had also given a fellow worker some candy and I asked her if she threw it away and she said, "I sure did," without even contemplating his generosity. I just wonder about the poor old man. He probably spends his begging money on candy, only to give it away and have it thrown away. Perhaps he's feeling guilty for something that happened years ago. Perhaps he's just a nice old person. Whatever the case, I can relate.

People talk about how mature they are and then they go out and destroy themselves. Maturity is reaching the point of dealing with problems with your mind and only your mind. How can someone be content if they are constantly fucked up? When they come down, their problems are there staring them right in the eyes. That's maturity? I don't think so.

People get down on others for being so sensitive and emotional. Who gives someone the right to taunt someone who cares? Sensitive and emotional people are the most caring, compassionate people around. And there is nothing wrong with crying. Crying is just a way to release unwanted feelings. Or, on the other hand, it can be a way of showing extreme happiness. I don't see why some people can't handle this outlet when they do things to release that are harmful.

Everyone, including myself, is so contradicting. It makes the world senseless. Nothing means anything.

21 July 1989
6:05 p.m.

I took a hit of Woodstock acid at 5:43 p.m. I'm now waiting for something. I don't know what yet. I took my vitamin C today—a lot—and ate two oranges too.

7:38 p.m.

OK, I'm tripping.

It's hard to write on mushy paper. Once again it's very intense and I'm listening to Xymox.

2:53 a.m.

OK, I thought I'd write to you for a while while I'm tripping. I just sent you a letter. It has a quote about pot and acid on the back. It's true. Once you've had them there's no life without them. Shit, ever since I first did acid I've been filling voids with vices. When I haven't been on drugs I've been thinking about them. It's scary because I see myself as innocent as the girl in *Go Ask Alice* and turning into some dazed druggie, but I can't help it.

To think that part of the reason that I even tried acid in the first place was to have something to write about. Why do you mean that much to me? Now I have so many people telling me to get off acid, but they just don't know. Well, my friends who have done it and tell me to stop are the ones who have had bad trips.

What am I to do now? We each have 2 more hits. Should I stop now? I don't want to and that, THAT is what scares the hell out of me. I don't want to stop. All I think about anymore is drugs and alcohol.

3:22 a.m.

The one thing I hate about acid is not being able to be comfortable. Sex on acid is a nightmare. (I just know that one will get me in trouble. I read everything to Jack and he'll be hurt, but how shall I explain?). Fuck it. I won't and I don't know why I'm telling you. You've probably done more acid than I ever will…Right now I feel as if this pen is just a blood vessel and I'm pouring out my heart and soul on to this paper. I know acid is no big deal, well, actually to me it is and I don't want to like it so much. I don't want to keep doing it, but look. I keep doing it. No one understands. I can see how people can freak out. I was looking at some of my artwork and I was thinking all of these negative things like, why should I live? Such an easy way out. I really don't want to die. Jack looks uncomfortable.

Jack & Me

Jack is on my bed now and we're both tired, but I don't want to waste a good trip while sleeping. Jack is falling asleep. I started this artwork and it's pretty cool.

3:44 a.m.

I'm at the point where I wish I could turn it off, sleep for a while and come back later. I have so much to do tomorrow. At some times everything seems like such a bother. But I like life, don't get me wrong.

I think I'm starting to come down, but I'm not quite sure. I have a tiny little cut on my arm and it feels like my whole arm hurts. Oh, I can't explain. I think I'm tired of thinking. I just want to go to sleep and wake up to sanity.

A while ago I thought I was coming down, but I'm still tripping hard. Things seem to be annoying me but I'm so awake I just want to finish this book and send it off to you. Who even knows if I'll start another. I should just have a trip book. No, I should just stop tripping. I wonder what PCP is like.

Shit, I hate when I have things to do on the day after I trip. I'm still tripping so hard.

4:37 a.m.

Sometimes when I'm tripping, I forget how to breathe. It's strange. Well, I hate to do this but I really have to get some sleep and Jack said he'd give me a massage so I'll talk to you later. I bet you didn't know that I'm somewhat dominant and I usually get my way. I'm not saying that I'm proud of it.

Oh, shit, you're going to think I'm insane but there is a whole other dimension in my eyelids. I swear. It's like I close my eyes and I'm in another world. I still know reality but I'm barely touching it. I thought my eyes were still open at first but I checked and they weren't. The visuals are so fucking excellent! I should've had my eyes closed the whole time. It's so wild, I can't even explain. I saw all of these rats running up a hill and I was watching them. They were all running to those treadmill things and I felt my eyes like they were going into the back of my head. I'm OK. I'm OK. Stay calm.

22 July 1989
1:23 p.m.

Hello. OK. I didn't get to sleep until around 6:30 this morning because I couldn't remember how to sleep and breathe at the same time. My eyes are still way dilated and I was supposed to go meet the general manager at my new job, but there is just no way I can with these glassy dilated pupils of mine.

I was so scared this morning.

On the bus to Oakland (Pittsburgh)

I'm at a very confusing stage of my life. Do drugs make you turn into the old man sitting next to me on this bus? Who in the world does he think he's speaking to? He's talking about Algeria and Commies. Shaking hands. He shook hands with him in Africa on duty. Everyone in the world. He saw him discover Antarctica. Who is this man? Was he once intelligent? Discover what? Does he know what he's saying? South Carolina out by Antarctica. He knows. Oh, he was in the service. Fuck. Is he reading my mind? Kids in college in Oakland. Whatever he's saying could be wrong. Fuck, he is reading my mind.

23 July 1989

Well, the other night I tripped and also got high. I'm getting scared because I think I like unreality way too much. It got really scary at the end. I was seeing so many visuals. I saw so many designs and skulls and rats and Jesus and kings and queens and frogs and everything. When I closed my eyes I thought they were opened, when I touched them I found that they weren't and then I wasn't sure which was reality. It was scary. I thought that I was going to remain that way forever…I was on a magic carpet and I was about to go into yet another dimension and I would stay there forever.

I thought I was never going to see the sane world again. I was convinced that I got like a quadruple hit and that I was going to be schizophrenic. I saw frogs mating on Jack's ceiling. I wanted so badly to talk to Bev (the girl that I got the acid from) because I wanted to ask her if she saw the other dimension when she closed her eyes. As soon as I thought about it she was there in Jack's room getting high with some guy.

We have 2 more cute little hits. They are in my desk drawer and I can take them whenever I want. Maybe I should sell them. I can get at least $10 for them. Wait, I just remembered that Jack paid for them anyway. Like you care, I'm sure. Anyway, I'm really beat so I'm going to get some sleep.

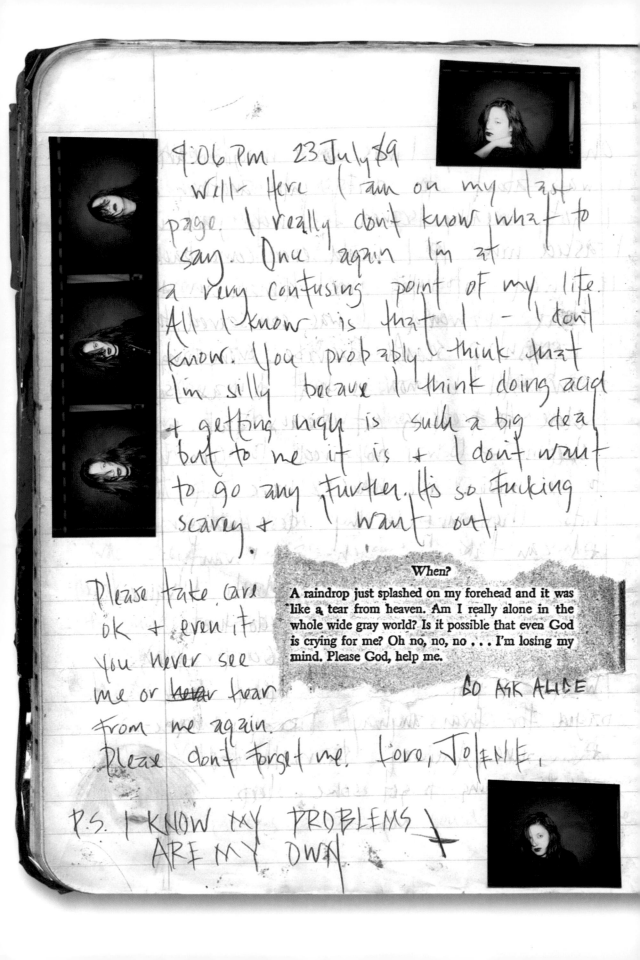

4:06 PM 23 July 89
Well Here I am on my last
page. I really don't know what to
say. Once again I'm at
a very confusing point of my life.
All I know is that I - I don't
know. You probably think that
I'm silly because I think doing acid
+ getting high is such a big deal
but to me it is + I don't want
to go any Further. Its so fucking
scarey + I want out.

Please take care
ok + even if
you never see
me or ~~never~~ hear
from me again.
Please don't forget me. Love, JOLENE.

P.S. I KNOW MY PROBLEMS
ARE MY OWN.

When?

A raindrop just splashed on my forehead and it was
like a tear from heaven. Am I really alone in the
whole wide gray world? Is it possible that even God
is crying for me? Oh no, no, no . . . I'm losing my
mind. Please God, help me.

GO ASK ALICE

8 November 1990 (Journal)

It's 12:07 a.m. I'm in Columbus, Ohio. I'm a happy kid drinking hot chocolate in a 24-hour place. Alone, waiting and waiting. It looks like I will be getting a ride with Skinny Puppy's truck driver. I've had the most wonderful week and it's only Wednesday. Technically Thursday. I have gotten many warm kisses this week. Friendly warm kisses from friends whom I admire.

Glenn picked me up and we proceeded to go to Columbus. We got there and found the Newport quite easily. We went over to the bus and Lenny knocked. Skully came to the door. I was very excited. I hugged him and we talked a bit. He asked if we were going inside and I told him that we didn't have tickets. He got the tour manager and he said he'd try to put us on the list and Skully said that he would pay if he couldn't. He hugged me and said he'd talk to me inside.

We went inside and I spoke to the T-shirt guy for a bit. I was creeping through the crowd and I noticed someone familiar and this someone noticed me and we stared at each other for a moment. It was Ogre and he said, "Jolene!" He smiled, held out his arms, and hugged and kissed me. He held me close to his side and kept asking how I'm doing. He seemed really happy, and just like last time he said, "You've grown up." I touched his hair and then touched mine and I said, "Look my hair's not black anymore." He smiled and said, "I know." He said, "I'm glad you're still around." I wasn't nervous or anything around him. It was so cool. I told him that I'm really embarrassed about some of the things that I've written and he was like, "Why? Don't be." He asked me what I've been doing and I said I've been keeping busy, coming up with a lot of ideas and dealing with my ex-boyfriend. He was like, "Believe me, I know what you mean. This past year...I could tell you a lot."

Then I said, "I have something really cool for you and I think you'll like it, but you'll have to wait until you play Pittsburgh," and he said, "What's that?" and I said, "A human skull," and I swear to God his eyes lit up like a child's eyes and he got this HUGE smile on his face and he fucking bowed to me. It was so cute. He seemed to be so happy.

I said that I feel like I could do a lot with my life because I have a lot to offer and he said, "Keep it up because what you're doing is some great shit." Then he said that he had to go back and he gave me another big hug and kiss on the cheek and said he'd see me after the show. After the show the tour manager gave us passes and we went backstage. Ogre was still all bloody and he was sitting next to Kat from Babes in Toyland. She was pretty drunk. Ogre said hi to me. Kat got up and Ogre said, "Jolene, sit down," and I said, "Where?" and he said, "Here, next to me." We spoke a bit and then he said, "I have to leave soon," and I said, "Where are you going?" and he said, "Back to the hotel to shower." He asked if I was going to Cleveland and I said yes. He said he would put me on the guest list and then he said goodbye.

I went outside and then went to get a hot chocolate with the wife of one of the crew members until the truck with the gear was about to leave. I got in (he offered me a ride) and we followed the bus to the hotel. I started to fall asleep in the front seat and this guy who was also riding with the truck driver said that it wouldn't bother him if I slept in the back cab (where he was sitting). He was bugging the hell out of me by trying to talk to me. I was tired. I proceeded to the back to sleep and I was pressed up against the wall. He put his hand on my waist. I pushed his hand away and said, "No, I don't think so." He said, "Oh, I'm sorry, I wasn't going try anything, I just want to cuddle." I just went back to sleep. He tried several times and I was getting really sick of it. The last time he tried it I was in the midst of a deep sleep. I was really pissed and I said, " I don't even know you and I want to sleep!"

I woke up to the sound of country music in my ear. I got up. It was about 10:20 a.m. or so. I went inside the club and called Jen. She wasn't home so I changed and cleaned up in the bathroom and got a ride downtown. I hung out in Tower City all day. I caught a bus back to the Agora. I saw Skully and we talked a bit. I told him about the asshole on the truck. He was mad and said that he was going to say something to him. I told him not to and he said that he was going to because no one does that to one of his friends. I was waiting in line before the show and I befriended these two girls, Jami and Lee.

Inside the Agora, Babes in Toyland had started. We went down in front, and as we were walking back I noticed Ogre in the audience again. I went over to him and he asked if I got here all right. I told him about he gross guy in the truck and he was surprised. I introduced him to Jami and I told him that I'd talk to him later. During Skinny Puppy, Gary let us sit on the balcony with him. After the show everyone got kicked out and Gary gave Jami a pass so we went backstage but the doors were closed. Dwayne was standing by the door and I asked him if he remembered me. He said, "Yes, Jolene or something." He took us around backstage and gave us beers.

Ogre was in the corner with a bunch of people. Jami and I went over and he asked me if I brought the skull and I said he'd have to wait until Pittsburgh. He said, "Cool." I asked he if I still had my own box and he said, "Of course you still have your own box!" He proceeded to tell these people about all of the letters that I had written and he was saying that he is going to call me years from now and that we would laugh and laugh and I was like, "No, think I'll just be really embarrassed," and he said, "No way, you wrote some cool shit!" And I said, "No, I didn't," and he said, "Yes, you did!" and I modestly said, "OK, I know I did," and he said, "You know you did!" I was so very flattered.

I was getting pretty drunk. Dwayne and cEvin kept asking me why I had my camera so we decided to take pictures.

We hung out on the bus for a long time. Dwayne kept teasing me about the guy on the truck. He said that Rave told him. Skully was in and out taking care of things.

Pittsburgh, PA

Ogre & Me

Skully & Me

Dwayne, Cevin, me & skully

SKINNY PUPPY

Dwayne Goettel

183

Ogre photographed by Me

I was pretty much drunk and I kept babbling. Ogre came out and hung out with us. I went in the back to get my bag from Skully. He hugged me and kissed me on the head. Then I went to the front and I was saying bye to Ogre. He hugged me and I said, "Don't forget," and he said, "I know, the pictures." And I said, "I'll bring the skull." He hugged me and said, "Jolene, Jolene, Jolene, Jolene." It was so affectionate and cute. Then he told me to bring Jami to the show. cEvin said, "Hey, Dwayne has a serious crush on Jami." Then I left. Just as we were almost to the car I realized that I forgot my purse so I ran back to the bus and grabbed it. Ogre was on the floor and Dwayne was on top of him. They were so messed up.

30 June 1991
3:28 p.m.
Dear Ogre,

Hi. How are you keeping? Hopefully well. I've been thinking about you lately.

Anyway, I'm a bored and unemployed art school graduate. I'm doing things like making beads (such as the one that I gave to you) and selling my boyfriend's acid just to get by. Though I have been interviewing and I also got myself a freelance job. I'm going against my morals and I'm not too happy about myself. I guess it's not that bad. I'm photographing a circus. Three shows in two days for $100. That's really not a lot for being a professional, but I can't be too picky these days. I'm interviewing for this job of traveling around to photograph college students. I guess it's good pay. The only thing is that I'd have to be away from Jack. I'd also have to purchase another car.

4 July 1991
Happy Independence Day.
Well, here I sit. I'm mad because Jack may not be back for a while. He may visit a friend in Wyoming. Yes, Wyoming. Whatever. Anyway, I did the freelance job that I told you about. It was all right. I got a hideous sunburn. It sucked because at one point there were animal rights activists outside of the circus handing out information on animal cruelty in circus. This guy that I met was wearing an anti-"Animal Rights Cults" T-shirt so of course I was offended. All the people that I met were really nice except for the owner but I still felt sorry for the animals. They had little pigs and goats and elephants and dogs (which they did rescue from a pound). They also had camels, donkeys, horses, peacocks, etc. Oh, they had lions and tigers that I felt the most sorry for because they had teeny, tiny cages. This guy told me that they do have a large winter quarter. Anyway, it was an experience and I had to do it because I'm broke. I did, however, get hired at a portrait studio. I'm still going to interview for the other company to photograph college students. So there.

Have you ever seen *Bad Taste*? It's a psycho movie that Jack and I watched once when we were on mushrooms. That was the strangest and last trip I ever had. I was separate from myself. I was out of it and Jack seemed to be convulsing. The reason that came up is because the movie that's on reminds me of *Bad Taste*. Anyway, I'm going to go.

Oh, the reason I wanted to write to you was to thank you for never making me feel stupid. You've always been so nice to me and I wanted to let you know that I really appreciate your kindness (That includes putting me on the guest list, etc.).

TAKE CARE OF YOURSELF.

Jolene M. Siana

May 2001 (Journal)

I took Bob to see "Ohgr" (Ogre's solo project) play at the Palace. I hadn't been to a show in a very long time. I hadn't seen Ogre in 9 years. I only found out about his new album earlier this month when I ran into cEvin Key at Danny Carey's birthday party. I had asked him to tell Ogre that I said hello.

Before the show I ran into cEvin in the parking lot. He told me that he passed my message onto Ogre and that he wanted to say hello to me.

The show was incredible. It really took me back. After the show I managed to find the tour manager and arrange getting backstage. It felt so awkward to me. I hadn't done that in ages.

Bob and I waited around for quite awhile. Ogre came out and people were crowded all around him. I was waiting for a time when he wouldn't be surrounded by fans, but I finally realized that I would not see that moment so I went up to him and tapped him on the shoulder. I said, "Ogre, it's Jolene." He said, "Jolene! I still have your letters." I was in shock.

He followed that with, "Remember that skull you gave me?" He was very warm and seemed happy to see me. He said that he had lost everything in his apartment but he managed to hold on to my letters. We exchanged email addresses and he promised to get the letters back to me.

June 2002 (Journal)

I ran into Ogre at the Dungeon the other night. He was standing in line. I was with Tracy and Marifrances. I saw him, but it didn't register until he called my name. We had had some email correspondence throughout the past year in regards to the letters. He told me that they were in Calgary and that he would work on getting them to me. We shared a drink inside. I told him that I was anxious for their return. He made it a point to tell me that he really hoped that writing them had helped me. He said that I scared him and that he was worried about me, but that he knew that I wouldn't kill myself. Having this conversation was surreal.

August 2002 (Journal)

I got my letters back from Ogre today! I heard the FedEx man coming up the stairs. I'm certain that he had no idea what kind of emotional energy was contained in that package—these letters, which have traveled from various locations in the Midwest to Ogre in Vancouver, then to Calgary, and finally back into my hands in Los Angeles.

Opening the box was intense, to say the least. I found 73 letters, 14 postcards, and 5 full notebooks intimately detailing my younger life. There were many unopened letters…artwork and words which had not been viewed, some sent 15 years ago. A lonely girl in her dark bedroom spewing thoughts of depression, insecurity and self-loathing. A girl with a passion to find herself.

I had forgotten a lot of the events that I'd written about. I phoned Ayse% and we spoke at length about the past. We marveled at how much we depended on each other back then. We spoke about how important music was to us, and remembered the times all of us pen pals got together. We thought about how cool it was that music was the common bond that drew us to each other.

Over the past few days I've become reacquainted with the girl I used to be. I've been taken to my bedroom that hasn't existed for 15 years. I've taken road trips to see bands that I haven't listened to in ages. I've recalled forgotten conversations with friends who helped to shape the person I am today. I've read about goals of the past that have come true. I've seen patterns in my behavior. I got my heart broken. I experimented with drugs. I laughed, I cried.

Probably the most shocking reminders of the past dealt with my suicidal thoughts and self-injury. I remember that I used to cut myself. I just didn't realize how often. I think part of the reason I forgot was that no one, including me, knew what cutting was back then—not even my therapists or counselors. All I knew was that it made me feel better. It was a release. Bloodletting. But I felt shameful doing it at the same time. I didn't discover until a few years ago how common self-injury is. Interesting as well is that most self-injurers come from dysfunctional homes like mine, are generally intelligent, and strive for perfection—just like me.

September 2002 (Journal)

I've been engrossed in the letters. It's been a very emotional few weeks. So many memories coming back to me. I really forgot about how much pain I was in. I'm glad Ogre didn't read all of them. He told me about this, and honestly, I'm thankful. I really poured a lot of heavy shit on him. I still can't believe I have these letters back in my hands. I can't believe he saved them for me.

Our family reunion is in a few weeks, so I made an appointment to see Bonnie (my therapist). The letters are opening some wounds and I really want to be able to go home without the anger and hurt affecting my time with my mother. I had never told Bonnie about these obsessive letters in the 3 years that I've been going to her. I took some of the letters and notebooks with me and she was floored. She was fascinated by the documents. She told me that she believed that these letters which, were clearly driven by pain, had very likely saved my life. I agree. I've been getting pretty emotional about it. It even brings me to tears. I don't want to be sad about it because I'm pretty happy now, but it's uncontrollable. It's something I just can't help.

31 December 2003
Los Angeles, CA (Journal)

"How do you feel about all of that now?"

It's New Year's Eve, 2003. I am standing in the kitchen of cEvin Key's home in the Hollywood Hills. I am speaking to Ogre. The reunion is a complete surprise to me, as I had no idea he would be here this evening. I'm lucky myself, as my only goal for the evening was to not be working in my restaurant at midnight. As it turns out, I made it to Bree and cEvins with 4 minutes to spare, and to my surprise, I was bringing in the New Year with Ogre, my former obsession. He is standing here saying things like, "Look at you now," and asking me, "How do you feel about all of that now?" He is referring to the letters that I wrote to him obsessively for roughly 3 years. So, how do I feel? All I can really think about is how excited I am about writing the book and how supportive he is. But really, how do I feel?

Did I have any idea when I was 17, alone in my room, alone in my life, reaching out to someone whom I'd never met, someone who I didn't even know much about, pouring out thoughts that I couldn't even share with my closest friends? Did I think he would respond? How could I know that I would eventually meet him? Did I have any clue that some 16 years later I would be hugging Ogre, bringing in 2003 in Los Angeles? How do I feel about all that? I think it's pretty fucking cool.

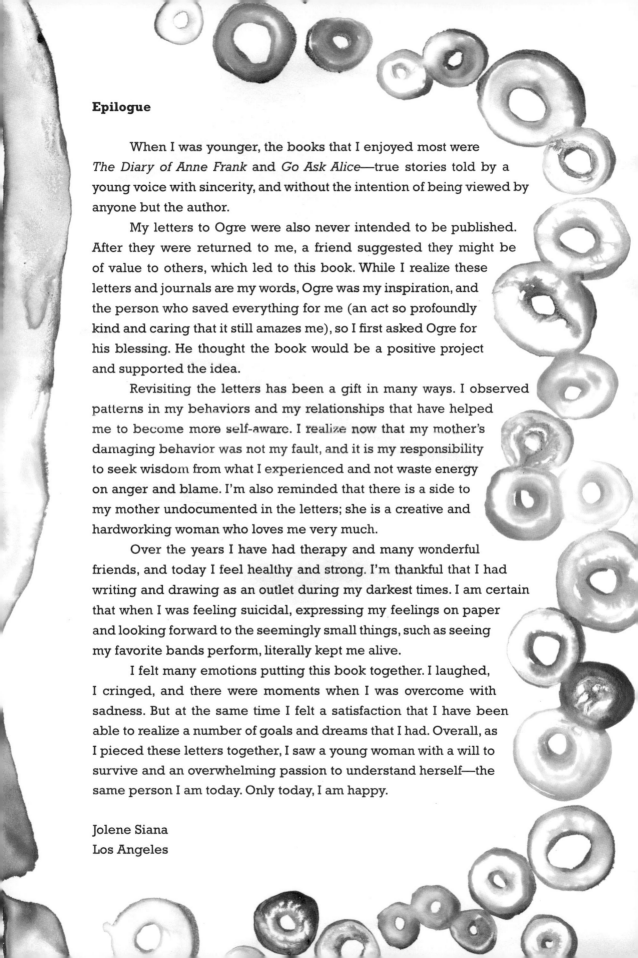

Epilogue

When I was younger, the books that I enjoyed most were *The Diary of Anne Frank* and *Go Ask Alice*—true stories told by a young voice with sincerity, and without the intention of being viewed by anyone but the author.

My letters to Ogre were also never intended to be published. After they were returned to me, a friend suggested they might be of value to others, which led to this book. While I realize these letters and journals are my words, Ogre was my inspiration, and the person who saved everything for me (an act so profoundly kind and caring that it still amazes me), so I first asked Ogre for his blessing. He thought the book would be a positive project and supported the idea.

Revisiting the letters has been a gift in many ways. I observed patterns in my behaviors and my relationships that have helped me to become more self-aware. I realize now that my mother's damaging behavior was not my fault, and it is my responsibility to seek wisdom from what I experienced and not waste energy on anger and blame. I'm also reminded that there is a side to my mother undocumented in the letters; she is a creative and hardworking woman who loves me very much.

Over the years I have had therapy and many wonderful friends, and today I feel healthy and strong. I'm thankful that I had writing and drawing as an outlet during my darkest times. I am certain that when I was feeling suicidal, expressing my feelings on paper and looking forward to the seemingly small things, such as seeing my favorite bands perform, literally kept me alive.

I felt many emotions putting this book together. I laughed, I cringed, and there were moments when I was overcome with sadness. But at the same time I felt a satisfaction that I have been able to realize a number of goals and dreams that I had. Overall, as I pieced these letters together, I saw a young woman with a will to survive and an overwhelming passion to understand herself—the same person I am today. Only today, I am happy.

Jolene Siana
Los Angeles

Afterword

> "In every child, no matter what the circumstances, and of no matter what parents, the potentiality of the human race is born again, and in him, too, once more and of each of us terrific responsibility toward human life, toward the utmost idea of goodness, of the horrors of error, and of God."
> — James Agee

The families we grow up in pass on unacknowledged pain from the families they grew up in. They also show us by example how to cope with our own pain. Ways of coping with pain can be constructive and useful, or they can be damaging and destructive. Most of us learn both.

When Jolene first came to me, her pain was partly manifested in her inability to find true connection in her relationships. She only knew how to be with people who were so absorbed in their own pain that they were abusive and unavailable to her. This was her family's pattern, the pattern Jolene had come to know as love.

Of the coping mechanisms Jolene acquired to deal with her pain, many became her strengths. Her writing, artwork, and ability to communicate and reach out have brought her a long way.

I believe there are no accidents. That the person she reached out to in her darkest times was touched by her letters is no accident. That he kept her letters intact through difficult circumstances is also no accident. That Jolene had the opportunity to face her past through her letters is nothing short of a miracle and a true gift.

I am touched by her courage. I am in awe of her perseverance and her spirit, and feel privileged to have been with her through a small part of her journey. I hope that Jolene's story helps to show others in pain that better ways are possible. Most importantly, I hope she continues on her path to find better ways for herself.

Bonnie B. McLaughlin, MA, MFT
Burbank, California

Resources

Al-Anon/Alateen
888.4.ALANON
(888.425.2666)
www.al-anon.alateen.org

Covenant House/Nineline
800.999.9999
800.999.9915 TTY
www.nineline.org

SAFE (Self-Abuse Finally Ends)
800.DONT.CUT
(800.366.8288)
www.selfinjury.com

Recommended reading

Bodies Under Siege: Self-Mutilation and Body Modification in Culture and Psychiatry by Armando R. Favazza, M.D. (Johns Hopkins University Press)

A Bright Red Scream: Self-Mutilation and the Language of Pain by Marilee Strong (Viking Press)

Cutting: Understanding and Overcoming Self-Mutilation by Steven Levenkron (W.W. Norton & Company)

The Luckiest Girl in the World by Steven Levenkron (Penguin)

Bodily Harm by Karen Conterio and Wendy Lader with Jennifer Kingson Bloom (Hyperion)

Skin Game: A Memoir by Caroline Kettlewell (St. Martin's Griffin)

Note: This list should be considered as a reference source only and is not intended to substitute for an individual's medical and/or psychological treatment. It is not the equivalent of, nor is it intended as a replacement for, any professionally supervised treatment. Process Packaging, Inc. disclaims any liability arising directly or indirectly from the use of this material.

Acknowledgements

A special thank you to Process: Adam Parfrey & Jodi Wille. It is an honor to be one of the first Process releases. Jodi, as my editor & publisher, thank you for sharing my vision, for your patience, guidance and all of your hard work.

Ogre, I am forever grateful for your kindness and support.

Aunt Karen, thank you for buying me paint brushes, journals, clothes, facials, manicures, etc., etc., and most of all, for being my biggest fan.

Mom, thank you for understanding why I needed to write this book, and for your encouragement and support along the way. Thank you for your creative flair, enthusiasm, and for giving me the gift of life.

To my entire family, thank you for allowing me to be the quirky black sheep…the one with many opinions…Thank you for understanding.

For 10+ years of friendship: Bob Fisher, Stephanie Huzaurewicz, Jack Kilby, Kimmy Lamse, Lori Mazuer, Gilden Tunador, Jodi Wille, I love you all & you make me love me! oXXo.

Much love & warm thanks for your support and for simply affecting me in one way or another…Karl Alvaraz, Angel (Fetisch), Jonathon Antalek, The Art Institute of Pittsburgh, Astridur, Milo Aukerman, Big Glenn, Blush, Uncle Bob, Brian & Kristy, Café Legendz (Patrick & Michelle), Donnie Campbell, Danny Carey, Sabine (Bientje) Carey, Celeste, Kim Colwell, Timothy Connors, Joanna Contreras (Red Star Ind.), Jenny Cousino, Jon Crosby, Carri (Psychee) Cuicani, D., Daily Grillers, Paul D'Amour, Felicia Daniel, Myra Davies, Dean, Jamez "de Bramski", Debbie Diamond, Stephen Egerton, Gregg Einhorn, Tricia Fetters, Shanti Fletcher, Yvonne Fraser, Tracy Gardner, Valerie Gatchell, Corey Goldberg, Greg, Gretchen, Dave Heisey, Barry Hennsler, Johnny Hoover, Jeroen, JK, Al Jourgensen, Christy Ju, Karen Keeler, Melissa Kelley cEvin Key, Mrs. Kroniviter, LA Graphico crew, Jeff Lightford, Ms. Lipe, Mackenzie, Natalya Madolora, Mark (Markie-Mark), Mary, Mr. McGrew, Bonnie McLaughlin, Josh Mills, Stacy Mohr, Mojca, Ronny Moorings, MySpacers, Aunt Nor Nor, David (Rave) Ogilvie, Frank Owen, Pepper (Pepé/Peppercini—you give the best doggie hugs), Jami Powers, Michael Quinney, Mr. Ramanowicz, Alan Rapp, Boomer Reynolds, Richard (Whooli) Roberts, Rocky Cola kids, Rosemary, Diane Rosen, Karine Rosenthal, Rachel S., Mr. Samples, Jon Schickedanz, Ana Schultz, Kevin Sciecinski, Lee Scuderi, Alex (Skully) Scull, Sherry & Ronny, John R. Shupe, Simon, Dave Smith, Nicole Smith, Jimmyjoe Snark III, Danny "Bug" Snow, Sparky, Jon Stainbrook, Bill Stevenson, Steffany Swendt, Todd Swalla, Viv Szabo, Tam Girls, Tanna, James Teitelbaum, Bree (Breezy) Thompson, Ayse (%) Tuzlak, Noelle Upchurch, Luc Van Aker, Jessie Waldamer, Johnny Weills, & Steve & Cheryl Wind.

Posthumous thanks to: Grandma & Grandpa, Anne Frank, Dwayne Goettel and Jane Nicklin.